DEAR T[illegible] LET'S TALK ABOUT PERIMENOPAUSE

Abimbola Gbemi Alao

First published in 2019 by Lampo Educational Services

ISBN 978-0-9546255-8-0

www.abimbolaalao.com

Dear Toriola

You shall flourish like a palm tree…
you will still bear fruit in old age;
you will stay fresh and green.
– Psalm 92

----- Original Message -----
From: Wura Francis <wurafrancis@hommie.com>
To: Toriola Oba <toriolaoba@nmail.com>
Cc:
Sent: 20 Oct 2012, 09:20
Subject: Congrats!

Dear Toriola,

I hope this email finds you well. Congrats once again on your 40th birthday. I'm so sorry I couldn't make it, but it was gracious of you to send me the link to your photos online. You look gorgeous! I'm so, so happy for you. I was glad to see Fikayo in the photos; I'm guessing you're back together.

It's been a long time, my dear, but my silence wasn't intentional; I've been through hell and back with my health. The past couple of years have been very challenging as I have battled joint pain, dizziness, insomnia, hot and cold flushes and lethargy, to mention but a few issues. It's a long story, but the good news is that I have overcome every debilitating symptom and I feel refreshed and more energetic than ever. After many months of suffering, I went to my GP and he suggested that, based on my age and my symptoms, the culprit may be perimenopause. Peri... what? I thought; I knew about menopause, but I didn't realise it has a precondition!

Anyway, please ignore my miserable story; that's not the purpose of this email. I am writing to wish you many happy returns, but I thought you should also know why I couldn't make it to Nigeria for your big day.

I pray this will be the beginning of better things for you, and you will experience great joy as you step into this new season of your life. Do write to let me know that you got my email.

I look forward to hearing from you.

Wura

----- Original Message -----
From: Toriola Oba <toriolaoba@nmail.com >
To: Wura Francis <wurafrancis@hommie.com>
Cc:
Sent: 27 Nov 2012, 02:00
Subject: Re: Congrats!

Dear Wura,

My darling sister from another mother! It was so good to hear from you. I am sorry I couldn't get back to you earlier; I was ill. I've been off work for a while, but I'm back part-time, not because I'm well, but because the bank is threatening to lay me off. As you can imagine, that means trouble, because I'm still the breadwinner. Yes, Fikayo is back, but as usual, one leg in, one leg out; nothing has changed. I'm only condoning his behaviour because my ears are full of gossip from friends and family… 'she can't even keep her home…' Yada, yada, yada …they go, nonstop. You know how it is here.

Anyway, the last thing I want to do is bore you with my problems. However, in your previous email, you mentioned something that got me thinking. It's about the symptoms you said you had. I am experiencing similar issues, but in addition, I have terrible palpitations and I am breathless every time I walk a few paces. I've been to three hospitals, but after taking all the drugs recommended to me, I feel worse. The hot flushes are a nightmare; the pressure on my head that announces the onset of a flush makes me feel awful.

You know Maami died at the age of 45, and I remember that my dad took her to many clinics and hospitals, and they couldn't even diagnose what was wrong with her. My friend, I am afraid, really afraid. I don't want to die young! I don't know what the problem is. Why am I feeling breathless? Why does my heart keep pounding like it is going to explode? They said I don't have a heart problem, but I don't trust these Nigerian hospitals.

In your email, you said that you overcame every debilitating symptom. My dear, I have some questions:

- I know you're not a medical doctor, but do you think my issues could be related to perimenopause, as you mentioned in your email? I'm an educated woman, yet I've never heard this word before. I know about menopause, but what is perimenopause?
- Were you diagnosed? I'm sure Oyinbo people can diagnose anything and everything. I'm not sure I could get a diagnosis for such a thing here in Nigeria.
- What did you do – I mean what steps did you take to find a cure or healing?
- Can you please send me information on what to do? Do you think I may also find a pathway to healing?

Wura, I'm desperate! If the bank eventually lay me off, what will happen to my kids, Remilekun and Maria? As you know, Fikayo has never been there for us. Please get back to me as soon as you can.

Love you loads!

Toriola

PS

I am having a lot of trouble with screen glare from the computer, so I'm avoiding it as much as possible, even at work. Could you write letters instead? I mean the good old snail mail. Our Lekki address hasn't changed. Thanks!

December 2012

Dear Toriola,

It was great to hear from you! I was worried when I didn't get a reply to my email after a few weeks. I thought perhaps you were angry that I didn't come to your birthday celebration. Unfortunately, I don't have your new mobile number. I tried the number that I used to call you on, but I didn't get through. Yes, of course, I'm happy to write letters to you instead of emails.

I'm so sorry to hear about your health issues. What an ordeal! I'll try to answer the questions you raised in your email. If you're experiencing the same symptoms that I mentioned earlier, including constant hot flushes, night sweats and dreadful mood swings, and the doctors are saying they can't find anything wrong with you, then you may be going through perimenopause.

I'm not surprised you haven't heard of it. Neither had I until my health deteriorated. It was only after I had my breakthrough that I began to ask women what they knew about perimenopause, and I was shocked to find that although many had heard of menopause, they didn't know anything about its 'prerequisite', if I may use that word. Even the few who said they'd heard of perimenopause did not realise it could disrupt a woman's life so much as to affect her mentally and physiologically.

One day I woke up drenched in sweat and my heart was palpitating like it was going to jump out of my chest. After several electrocardiograms (ECGs) and weekly trips to my doctor, I was told there was nothing wrong with me. I was mortified. There had to be something wrong with me. My heart kept pounding with such force it felt like when you beat yam with a pestle and mortar!

Subsequently, I suffered a whole host of unrelenting symptoms, and I had no clue why. Until that time I'd never heard of the 'P' word. I was 43 years old, but I didn't know there was such a thing as perimenopause and that it could cause physical and mental trauma. Like you, I was afraid. Fear made the situation worse because it bred anxiety.

To answer your second question, I wasn't diagnosed with perimenopause, although my gynaecologist suggested it may be the cause of my issues. When I got tired of the ceaseless trips to my doctor's surgery, I started doing my research and found out about perimenopause and the associated symptoms.

Some women, I learned, may not experience a single symptom during perimenopause, but others suffer debilitating symptoms that deprive them of vitality and affect their physical and mental wellbeing. In our modern world, where many people have stressful lives, eat poorly and rarely exercise, women increasingly see the symptoms of perimenopause early in their lives, some in their 30s and early 40s. Unfortunately, many of these women do not know what to do. At such a young age, perimenopause is the last thing on their minds, and there is so little support.

Unfortunately, I couldn't find anyone to help me navigate the treacherous labyrinth of perimenopause research, so I bought into an age-old lie: that the symptoms were natural, part of another stage in a woman's life – a rite of passage that every woman will go through. The question is, how do you fight something natural, something that is meant to be? The simple answer is, you can't. That's the lie women have been fed for centuries. A woman is made to believe that she should grit her teeth and endure whatever misery comes, just as she has endured her monthly cycle for years. However, there is nothing natural about vertigo, memory loss or flushes that make you sweat and shiver like someone plagued with malaria, and there is no good reason why women should suffer such horrendous symptoms in silence.

In my next letter, I will explain more about perimenopause. I had the early signs at just 36 when my period became erratic and the 'red flow' was heavy. My gynaecologists suggested surgery, ranging from ablation to a hysterectomy. Thank God I did not heed their advice. I was eventually placed on tranexamic acid, which I dutifully swallowed every month, during my period, for more than six years until I felt I'd had enough and began my search for natural ways to relieve my symptoms. There are natural treatments. People around you, including doctors, may tell you to live with your symptoms because they are natural. However, you don't have to go through trauma just because your ovaries are preparing for their retirement. There are ways to manage your body and get it ready for this time of your life.

I promise to write to you regularly, and yes, Toriola, I do believe that you too will find a pathway to health.

Much love,

Wura xx

January 2013

Dear Toriola,

Happy New Year! I pray this year will bring healing and joy to you. I hope you had lots of fun and a restful break. I had a quiet Christmas, no script marking and no course preparation. I think the decision I made to take a year's sabbatical is a good one.

I rarely make New Year's resolutions, but I decided that this year I will take long walks, if not daily then at least four times a week. I also decided I will go on retreats to rest and be refreshed; that is why I'm taking a short holiday to Arvon in Devon, which is where I'm writing this letter to you.

Yesterday I walked around the beautiful countryside, and the air was crisp and fresh. I am so grateful that I no longer have panic attacks, so I can walk for hours and enjoy the scenery. A few months ago, the story would have been different. I would have walked for about five minutes before hurrying back home. Yesterday I walked for more than an hour.

As I was about to enter the little cottage where I am staying, I saw a cow staring at me from a nearby field. She moved closer to the fence as if to acknowledge my presence, but as soon as her nose touched the fence, she turned around and walked away leisurely, swinging her tail from side to side. She soon resumed grazing, savouring every blade of grass without a care in the world. She chewed contentedly as if grateful for what she had at that moment, knowing tomorrow would take care of itself. As I was about to retire to bed, I remembered the cow and I gave thanks for the day and prayed that tomorrow would bring good things.

Perhaps being close to nature this week is sending my imagination into a higher frequency, because here I am, the next morning, writing to you. I didn't intend to write today, I just wanted to walk, pray and meditate, but I couldn't resist the urge to pen another letter to you.

In your last letter, you said you were worried that your health may not improve. I have been through a similar situation and the fear is real, my friend. However, I learnt something at the very onset of my deliverance from health issues and I will share this with you now:

One day, I went out to go to my local corner shop, which is about five minutes from our house. I'd only been walking for a couple of minutes when I suddenly felt a wave of cold flush, followed by intense pressure in my head and an ensuing panic attack. I turned around quickly and headed back. When I got home, I was so frustrated that I collapsed on the floor in tears.

'When, oh Lord, will I be set free? This is too much for me to bear; I have had enough!' I yelled.

That day, I couldn't eat much. All I could think about was the episode I had suffered during my walk. I went to bed early, and as I was about to fall asleep, a thought came to me: *'Your body is a living organism with ears; speak life to it'*. I sat up! It was as if a teacher was standing in front of me, giving me a detailed explanation. *'Your body responds to whatever word, thought or emotion you present to it because the difference between "true" and "false" means nothing to the body'*, the teacher said.

Prior to having this revelation, my mind had been consumed by how ill I was. Since I'd begun ploughing through the mire of perimenopause, every minute of the day was a nightmare. I sweated profusely and constantly felt dizzy and tired. I had frequent panic attacks and dreaded walking, so I stayed indoors most of the time – and the lack of exercise and fresh air exacerbated my health problems. I couldn't help sharing my stories of woe with anyone who cared to listen, and the more I complained about my situation, the worse it became. But that voice of a teacher in my mind made me realise: my body is like good soil that absorbs every thought and word, and it gives back an abundance of all that I plant in it.

Before I continue writing about the things I learnt from this revelation, I'd like to pause here and share a story with you.

Story: The Accident

One Friday evening, Mrs P was expecting her husband to come home for the weekend. He worked several miles away. That dark, stormy night, she tucked her two children into bed and was about to make herself a cup of tea when the doorbell rang. She hurried to the door to open it, but instead of her husband, there stood two policemen whose raincoats were dripping with water all over her porch.

'We're very sorry, madam', one said, 'but there has been an accident. We're so sorry to tell you that… that… he did not make it. Is there anything we can do for you? …

Madam, are you okay'?

The policemen called for an ambulance; Mrs P had passed out on the wet floor by their feet.

Later, at the hospital, Mrs P regained consciousness, but as she opened her eyes, she saw a man standing by her bed and, strangely, he looked like her dead husband. She rubbed her eyes vigorously, sat up in bed and let out an ear-bursting scream. Then she passed out again.

Later, when she opened her eyes, two nurses were holding her and the man was still standing by her bed. The nurses were very gentle…

'No, Mrs P, you're not hallucinating… No, you're not dead and in heaven; you're very much alive with us here… Yes, you're right; it is your husband… No, he's not dead. There was a mistake… So sorry, Mrs P, the policemen should have gone to number fourteen Torrent Street, but the storm was so bad and it was very dark, so they ended up at the wrong address… Yes, your address, number fourteen Torrent *Road*'!

In this story, it didn't matter whether the information that the police gave to Mrs P was right or wrong. Although they had come to the wrong address and her husband was not the accident victim, when she heard the news, her mind processed it, grief set in immediately and her body went into shock.

What point am I making here? Habitually, human beings retell past stories to themselves repeatedly. Through repetition, images of past events are firmly imprinted in the mind. Here's the good news; you can change an old narrative and create a new one that you want to see in the future. A new narrative, good or bad, influences your wellbeing. The body does not know the difference between what is true or what is false. It doesn't know whether an event has happened or not. It only responds to whatever the mind feeds it. As you tell your mind a new story, for example, a narrative of health and vitality, the body responds.

Once you've created a new narrative in your mind, it is

time to tell the story out aloud. Why are words so powerful? Let's examine the creation story as narrated in the book of Genesis: 'And God said, "Let there be light", and there was light… And God said, "Let there be an expanse in the midst of the waters, and let it separate the waters from the waters" and it was so… And God said, "Let the earth sprout vegetation, plants yielding seed, and fruit trees bearing fruit" And it was so'. We are told that before those creative words brought forth life, the earth 'was without form and void, and darkness was over the face of the deep'. However, God DID NOT speak about the chaos or void; rather, He spoke of what He wanted to see.

My point here is that, similarly, you can speak order over chaos, and life over death. It's no use talking of the negative things happening to you or around you. Instead, speak about the healing you want to see, because your body is listening to your words and you will see a manifestation of what you are saying.

This is not to say you should live in denial; if you do not feel well, see your doctor and get a diagnosis. I know you said you've already been to the hospital and have taken the necessary steps to seek help. Now you must change your focus from seeing yourself as a 'sick' person. See yourself as a healthy woman who is experiencing some challenges but is on the way to recovery. There is a big difference between the two.

We both know the importance of air; we cannot survive without it. Lack of oxygen for a few minutes can cause damage to the brain or even death. We also know the importance of water and how it hydrates the body and keeps our organs functioning well, and we know that nutrients from food are essential for the body. However, many people do not know the importance of words and how their bodies respond to every word they speak.

I struggled to speak positive words. When I had panic attacks and anxiety, all I could think about was how I felt. I was in a fearful state all day long, so how could I speak of anything different? I thought I was being truthful, but that wasn't the truth. The truth was that I was experiencing an affliction. As I prayed, my focus quickly changed from seeing myself as ill to seeing myself as healed.

Initially, it was challenging to do this, but one day, as I read from the book of Proverbs, I came across these words: 'The tongue has the power of life and death, and those who love it will eat its fruit.' I then decided to connect with life, so that I could eat the fruit of life.

That night, I realised my 'teacher' was right; my body is a living organism. Once I understood the lesson, I put it into practice. Now, each day when I wake up, irrespective of how I feel, I speak to my body. Here's what I say: 'Wura is my name and it means gold. Gold is a precious jewel; I am precious. Therefore, I decree that my body is whole, and it prospers even as my soul prospers. Amen'!

My dear Toriola, I would encourage you to think about the lesson I've shared with you in this letter and apply it. I hope it works for you as it has worked for me.

I am really enjoying writing to you and I look forward to sending you another letter soon. I also look forward to hearing from you. Do let me know if the messages in my letters are helpful.

Remember that your body is a living organism with ears. Speak life to it.

Much love,

Wura xx

February 2013

Dear Toriola,

How are your children, Remilekun and Maria? I saw Maria's Facebook request last week and I've accepted it. Wow, doesn't she look just like your mum? What a beautiful young woman. She shared her 16th birthday party pictures and she looked stunning. Also, as for Remilekun, hmmm… he's a younger version of your husband, Fikayo!

My dear, well done! You are doing so well with the children, despite all your difficulties. I've asked Ade, my daughter, to link up with Maria on Facebook. I've always wanted my Ade to be in contact with a responsible young girl back home so that she learns our values and culture. I do my best here in England, but I feel she may be more open with someone her own age. I'm so excited to hear about Remilekun's admission to uni, too. Give him my best wishes.

I am happy that you found the information in my last letter useful; thanks for your feedback. I'm glad that I could help and share the knowledge that I've gained on my journey.

Today I will answer the question you asked in your letter: 'What is perimenopause'? Before I explain further, I want to write a little about menopause. I'm sure you know about menopause, but I am mentioning it here so you can gain a better understanding of perimenopause.

What is menopause?

As a woman grows older, her ovaries produce fewer eggs. Gradually, a woman's monthly period winds down, until the ovaries stop sending eggs to the fallopian tubes and the woman ceases to menstruate.

The age when this happens varies greatly from woman to woman, and, for some reason, from country to country. For example, in the United Kingdom, the average age of menopause for women is fifty-two, and in the US it is fifty-one, while one in five women in India experiences menopause before the age of forty-one.

Menopause can happen in three different ways:

1. Artificially: due to damage to or surgical removal of the ovaries, chemotherapy or hysterectomy (smoking can also play a part).
2. Prematurely: when a woman goes through menopause before the age of 40.
3. Naturally: when a woman experiences it between the ages of 45 and 55. When menopause occurs between the ages of 40 and 45, this is called early menopause.

Now, let's go back to your question.

What is perimenopause?

Women do not just wake up one day to find they have entered menopause. The period just before menopause is called perimenopause, which means 'around the time of menopause'. The length of perimenopause varies from woman to woman. Some start to see signs in their mid to late 30s, while for others it can be mid to late 40s. One of the symptoms of perimenopause is an erratic menstrual cycle with heavy bleeding.

Hormones and perimenopause

Some medical scientists say that perimenopause is triggered by low oestrogen, while others say that high oestrogen could be responsible for many of the symptoms. Others argue that an imbalance of oestrogen, progesterone and testosterone and an abundance of synthetic xenoestrogen (a type of xenohormone that imitates oestrogen) triggers the issues that women face during perimenopause.

In 2004, the American Centers for Disease Control and Prevention conducted tests on more than 2,500 people and they found unmetabolised BPA in the urine of more than 93 percent of the subjects. In addition to BPA, phthalates and polychlorinated biphenyl are other examples of synthetic xenoestrogen that can imitate the effects of natural oestrogen and cause disorders of the reproductive system.

Hormonal imbalance causes a woman's body to throw tantrums. This can manifest in various ways: night sweats, hot flushes, vaginal dryness, breast tenderness, insomnia, irregular heartbeat, memory lapse, thinning hair, vertigo, tinnitus and anxiety, to name but a few. Many women experience physiological and psychological trauma during perimenopause and this can affect all aspects of their lives. The severity of the symptoms that precede menopause varies from woman to woman, but certainly some women suffer very badly indeed. Sadly, though, such trauma is not even recognised as a condition, let alone an illness.

Genes and perimenopause

Is a woman's experience of perimenopause hereditary? There isn't enough evidence to show what role genes play in when and how a woman experiences perimenopause and menopause. Writer Sarah Klein shared the views of Dr Margery Gass on perimenopause. According to Dr Gass, when it comes to actual symptoms, genetics isn't a strong predictor. Just because your mother had a difficult experience does not mean that you necessarily will.

It is possible that genetic factors determine the timing of perimenopause. However, there is no evidence to show that the numerous symptoms associated with it are hereditary. I will send you links to some helpful articles and books later. Whatever triggers perimenopause – grief, in my case – smooth sailing is still possible if you are well informed and adequately prepared for it.

I remember in my secondary school, our biology teacher held a class on menstrual cycles and hygiene. Unfortunately, I had started my periods already and had gone through the woes of not knowing why I was bleeding every month and whether it was going to continue forever. Nevertheless, for those girls who hadn't started their periods, the class provided valuable information and they were able to go through their experiences without the fear caused by ignorance.

Apparently, there are two types of perimenopause, the natural and the unnatural. I will share my understanding of these with you in my next letter.

Sending you warm hugs.

Much love,

Wura xx

March 2013

Dear Toriola,

I got your letter last night. I am glad you are getting so much out of the information that I'm sending to you. As promised, here is my understanding of the two types of perimenopause.

Natural perimenopause

This is the season when a woman's body prepares to end the menstrual cycle. It could be a time of erratic monthly bleeding, which eventually eases off and stops completely at menopause. Just as it is natural for a girl to enter puberty and start menstruating, so it is natural for a woman to stop menstruating.

God's plan is that the season of menopause is a time to celebrate being a mature woman. It is a time to flourish mentally, emotionally, creatively and physically. It is a time when a woman does not have to think of the discomfort of monthly bleeding or be afraid of getting pregnant, especially after a long period of child-bearing and selfless labour of love. I enjoy reading this verse, found in the 92nd Psalm and attributed to King David, the ancient psalmist. 'The righteous will flourish like a palm tree… they will still bear fruit in old age, they will stay fresh and green.'

God's plan for a woman is that she will flourish and remain

fresh. Sadly, the stories of many women who are going through menopause are very different from what God designed for them. My story was also one of woe because of the stressful situation brought about by perimenopause. However, I discovered the real story about this season of my life, and I embarked on a personal journey to know more when I realised there are two types of perimenopause.

Unnatural perimenopause

Many women today are experiencing an unnatural version of perimenopause, whereby their bodies, laden with viral, emotional and psychological toxins, built up over many years, are breaking down like an overused vehicle that refuses to go another mile. Unfortunately, the medical community to which they turn for help offers little relief. What many doctors offer is the age-old narrative that perimenopausal symptoms are natural and that there isn't much a woman can do, other than taking Hormone Replacement Therapies (HRT) that could potentially harm her body.

It is NOT the plan of the Creator that after a woman has gone through the discomfort of monthly bleeding for decades, and in many cases given birth to and raised children, she then hits another period of physical and mental distress.

One of the reasons people don't take perimenopause complaints seriously is because a woman's pain tolerance is high. After all, many of us have gone through painful period cramps and labour pain; surely we can endure a bit of sweating, madness and dizziness. It shouldn't be that way.

We are meant to enter this season victoriously. I love the verse in Psalm 139:16, 'all the days ordained for us are already written in God's book before our first day on earth and His thoughts to us are precious'. Notice the phrase 'all the days ordained for us'. This includes childhood, the teenage years, young adulthood, middle age and old age. His thoughts for these different stages of our lives are precious. Now I ask you, what is so precious about migraines, chronic pain, memory loss and constant hot and cold flushes?

The stories we have been told are contrary to the one that the master storyteller has written about us. In the Bible, a prophet called Jeremiah describes the Creator's plans for humans (29:11): '"For I know the plans I have for you," declares the Lord, "plans to prosper you and not to harm you, plans to give you hope and a future."' The hope and future that God has promised you are that you'll flourish as you age.

I am not attributing the word disease to perimenopause; however, for some women, their predicament is worse than a disease. Doctors may be able to diagnose and find a cure for a disease; not so with perimenopause. It has the potential to render a woman's body weak and susceptible to other illnesses. Some diseases, such as heart disease, affect an area of the body, so doctors focus on treating that. However, for some women who are going through perimenopause, their entire system is affected. They experience palpitations (cardiovascular), acid reflux (digestive), erratic menstrual cycles (endocrine), lethargy (immune), osteoporosis (musculoskeletal), panic attacks and depression (nervous) and certain allergies (respiratory). These symptoms can affect their daily routines and social lives.

Despite these problems, many women are not interested in Hormone Replacement Therapy, and neither do they want to be guinea pigs for new 'mood enhancement' drugs. They just want to have their lives back and enjoy their work and families.

At the age of 36, when my period became troublesome and my menstruation was like water dripping from a tap, I became so anaemic that my doctor had to place me on iron tablets and tranexamic acid. Initially, I thought there must be other options apart from taking medicines, but unfortunately, the only options I was given were surgical procedures, which I declined. I did not know that erratic menstrual flow was just the tip of the iceberg. I didn't know that I was about to enter a nightmare season.

Looking beyond hormones for the answer

Do all women experience unnatural perimenopause? The answer is NO. However, in our modern world where people have too much stress in their lives, are plagued with undiagnosed viral infections and indulge in unhealthy eating habits, many more women are struggling with their health. I don't believe that modern medicine understands how to deal with unnatural perimenopause. Hormones are labelled as the culprit, but is it all about the hormones? I think we need to start digging deeper than the 'hormonal' level for answers.

On my journey through the unnatural perimenopause, I discovered that some of the symptoms generally associated with hormonal imbalance could be due to viral infection, especially when the body has been under the attack of viruses that incubate over a long period before manifesting.

My dear friend, as you know I am not a scientist, and neither am I a medical doctor, but I have my own healing story to tell. My journey was a long one because I wanted to get to the root of my issues, and so I asked questions. As soon as I worked on healing my gut, many of the so-called perimenopause symptoms disappeared! My immune system, which was not functioning at its best, became strengthened and my body fought off viral infections and pathogens.

Increasingly, younger women will start experiencing conditions that used to be associated with old age. Hence it is essential to understand that hormonal imbalance is not the whole truth about a woman's journey through perimenopause and that this transition period can be smooth if you know the pathway to a trouble-free journey. My dear, from what you've told me about your symptoms, I think you may be experiencing the unnatural form of perimenopause. However, the good news is that there is a way out.

Please let me know if this information is helpful to you. I look forward to writing to you again.

Do keep well and be happy.

Much love,

Wura xx

April 2013

Dear Toriola,

I'm happy to hear that the bank is no longer threatening to lay you off. That news was like a great birthday present for me this month! Thanks for sharing with me in your last letter how much you appreciated my explanation of the two types of perimenopause.

In this letter, I will focus on your question about how and when perimenopause starts. The simple answer is that it differs from woman to woman. Every woman's journey and life experiences are unique. I will share my own story of how I entered the season of perimenopause, albeit the unnatural type. Please know that I am not making any claims about how the season of perimenopause is supposed to manifest.

If a woman is healthy, physically, emotionally and spiritually – which is rare in our present world – then she may not experience these horrible symptoms. However, if a woman is plagued with viruses, deadly bacteria, emotional and psychological issues, pathogens and other toxic waste, then the body may break down under the strain and stress of toxic overload. She may then be told that her hormones are rising and dipping like sea waves and that she is perimenopausal.

Unfortunately, some of the viruses that plague our bodies are patient as well as deadly. They may lie low in the organs for decades, looking for opportunities to strike when a person experiences emotional issues or illness. An example of such a virus is the Epstein-Barr Virus (EBV) that can incubate in the body for decades and then show its ugly face when the body is going through stress.

Let me share my own story with you:

As you know, I lost my mum three years ago. I think that was the last time I saw you – at my mum's funeral. However, because I had to travel back to the UK almost immediately after the burial, we didn't have time to get together.

I had only recently visited Nigeria. My mum had been excited to see me and we went to a few places together, but I noticed she had a slight limp. She put it down to a fall she'd had a few months earlier and said everything was fine. Unfortunately, she became weaker and the limping went from bad to worse, so I took her to the hospital.

She was admitted to the hospital and I told her I was going to cancel my flight, but she insisted that I travel back as initially planned. I boarded the plane early on a Tuesday morning, still very worried about her because she had experienced four fainting spells that weekend alone. I arrived in England late on Tuesday night, and on Wednesday morning I got a call from Nigeria to say that her condition had deteriorated and she was in a coma.

In the early hours of Thursday morning, at about one a.m., I awoke from a terrible dream. I was in a pit and bombarded by large insects, and though I tried to fight them off, they kept attacking me. I woke up drenched in sweat. It was so bad that my husband and I had to change the pillowcase and bedding. That was the first time I experienced a full night sweat.

At midday on the same day, I received a call from Nigeria

to tell me that my mother had passed away during the night – at one a.m. I was devastated. My mum was my best friend; it is difficult to put into words the special bond I had with her. Since my father died in 2004, we had grown even closer and she had become my prayer partner. She understood my gifts with dreams and visions, and I always felt at ease whenever I prayed with her. I called her nearly every day and we prayed over the phone.

At that time, I honestly did not know if I would ever recover from the grief. As usual, I bottled everything up, smiling and playing the 'big sister' to my siblings and making sure they were okay. However, I was sinking into the deep ocean and no one noticed.

Needless to say, I went through the stages of grief: shock, denial, pain, guilt, anger, sadness and loneliness in a rollercoaster. I was like a woman who'd been hit by a lorry, but instead of staying still and waiting for help, I'd got up, bleeding and confused, and carried on walking. After my mum's death, I plunged myself into work, even though I was still suffering emotionally. I was angry at everything and everybody whom I felt had 'allowed' my mum to die. I felt the doctors could have done a better job and saved her. I even thought perhaps if my siblings had taken better care of her then she may still be alive.

Before my mum's death, I had been experiencing very mild hot flushes, where I'd suddenly feel warm around my chest and face and I'd peel off a layer of clothing. At that time, I didn't know what was happening to me. I thought I was reacting to paracetamol because it seemed to happen when I took pain relief. However, starting the night that my mum passed away, I began to have full-blown flushes that came with a host of other symptoms like dizziness, head pressure, an incredibly fast heart rate and a general sense of malaise. The hot flushes increased in severity and frequency until I thought I was losing my mind.

One day, I woke up to a terrible sensation. It was as if someone had tied a rope tightly around my head and then put a large object on top of it. The worst experience was a strange feeling as if creepy crawlies were moving around inside my head. It was a nasty, painful sensation from the back of my head to the front. Once the pressure started, dizziness and blurry vision followed, and all I could do was sit down for a few minutes. The nasty head pressure became my miserable companion; it went everywhere with me, day and night, for several months.

I remember one night I was so frightened that I called the emergency services twice because I was in a terrible state and thought I would collapse at any moment. I was having hot and cold flushes, sometimes within a few seconds of each other, and dizziness compounded the problem. Thankfully, the emergency services were helpful and they managed to calm me down.

When I failed to get any relief, I went to see my doctor and he arranged for me to have a blood test. The results showed that everything was normal, except for anaemia. However, I didn't get better, and I felt lost and helpless in the treacherous labyrinth. I became a regular visitor to my GP, but most times all I got was a patronising smile and what felt like a little pat on the back.

Another malady I suffered from was panic attacks. During the attacks, I felt like I had stepped out of my body and was observing myself from a distance. These episodes came over me like dark waves and I felt helpless. I lost my appetite, became very sad for no apparent reason and felt like the world was a gloomy place that made me fearful and anxious.

I became an ardent internet surfer and found out that the symptoms I'd been battling came neatly packaged under the name of perimenopause. The internet provides a haven where people can be anonymous; not many women want to discuss perimenopause issues face to face.

I found numerous stories online. There were suggestions of holistic approaches, HRT, creams and drugs. However, one minute I'd be reading success stories of a product, and the next I'd find a hundred negative stories about the side effects of the same product. Some people swear by plant oestrogens, but there are also dangerous side effects to look out for. An example is black cohosh, which I used at one point; it helped to reduce the severity of the flushes, but it has side effects, such as visual disturbances and nausea. I tried some other natural plant products, but found no relief; rather, the pressure in my head and the dizzy spells became worse and a few disturbing thoughts began to race through my mind.

Soon I found myself slipping into a mire of despondency. Then I decided that enough was enough: I needed deliverance and I was going to get it. The first thing I learnt on the journey was that perimenopause should not be synonymous with physical and mental degeneration. It is more the case that the ups and downs of life and the various traumatic experiences that we women go through cause the body to react negatively.

You don't need to travel far to see that the world has only recently started to give women a chance to express themselves. Even today in many societies women are still treated as second-rate people who have no voice. When a woman tries to be assertive, she may be labelled aggressive. People even make mean jokes about a woman's menstrual cycle.

Some women go through physical, mental and emotional abuse in their homes, but they may be ashamed to tell anyone. They believe they are alone in their plight, or that something must be wrong with them. Some women see couples holding hands and going out together, and then they look at their relationship, which is falling apart, and think that they can make it work if they work harder.

A woman may have to deal with unruly teenagers, while it seems everyone else is managing to raise 'saints' who are doing well in school or university. She may turn to the man in her life for support, but get only grunts from him, and then she has the added stress of dealing with the in-laws.

Women can often be undermined, used, underpaid and unappreciated. Despite all these issues, they manage a smile under the layers of powder and mascara and get on with things. Anger, hatred, jealousy and fear of the unknown creep in, but these toxins are usually left unchallenged because people believe life is easier when they turn a blind eye.

Relationship problems, whether a person is married or single, can be a source of emotional upheaval. A woman whose husband cheats may find it difficult to articulate her pain. One woman who was suffering from high blood pressure described her husband's infidelity to me as follows: 'It's a man thing; that's how they all are. A woman has to get on with her life'.

This woman gets up every morning and carries on despite her situation; she doesn't want to rock the boat. That's a classic attitude of many women, but they do not realise that they are not 'getting on with life'; rather, they are stuck in their fears and worries. Interestingly, many of these women are breadwinners in their families, but the callous claws of fear hold them bound and they can't imagine breaking away from the abuse.

Unfortunately, negative emotions that are not addressed have a way of building toxic waste in the body. Women need to address them one by one, instead of brushing them under the carpet, because there is a day of reckoning. Storing up negative emotions for years is a pathway to ill health. You can get away with it when you're younger, but as you grow older the body makes demands on you and challenges you to start dealing with your thoughts and emotions or suffer the consequences.

Digging deeper into the root

When I began to understand that negative emotions are toxic, I prayed for wisdom on how to get to the root of my problems. One day, I was on my bed doing deep-breathing exercises – one of the things I've learnt to do to de-stress – and I saw myself as a nine-year-old, taking my siblings to school. I could almost see the anxiety on my face as I entered the school gates.

I am the eldest child, and from an early age I had the responsibility of looking after my siblings. I grew up in Nigeria, of course, where it is customary for the older sibling to take care of the younger ones. We had nannies occasionally, but most of the time I took my siblings to school and even made simple meals for them when we got back home. At school, if someone tried to beat them up, I would intervene quickly, even though I knew I could easily be overpowered. I was afraid of bullies, who took my money and sometimes beat me up, but I dared not tell my parents. That was the foundation of my fears and anxiety. Though it may seem subtle and insignificant, the foundation was firmly laid, and what I did over the years was to build upon it.

As the years went by, worry became my negative, toxic emotion. If my siblings didn't have enough money, I'd provide it, just so that my parents wouldn't worry too much. If they were ill, I would experience similar symptoms. Whatever challenges they had, we were in it together. I worried about my parents, my siblings and, eventually, my children. I was on an unending rollercoaster of worry.

In 2004, an unexpected tragedy occurred. My father, who had been ill for a few months, died at the age of 66. I didn't see it coming at all; he had been so healthy and agile. My father was a noble man and I loved him very much. He taught me everything I knew about integrity and being trustworthy; he was a fine gentleman. My mother was barely able to cope with her grief – they had been so close. Therefore, I had to bury my grief and look after her and be there for my siblings.

A few months after my father died, I became lactose intolerant and developed an egg allergy. Until that time, I'd happily eaten dairy and eggs, but a few months after my father's death, I couldn't eat these foods, and this continued for the next ten years.

It was six years after my father died that my mum passed away, at the age of 73. I hadn't even recovered from my father's death. I was devastated that these two fine people had died. My faith took a nosedive, mainly because I'd prayed for their healing and yet they still died. But again, I had my siblings to look after; I could not afford to break down.

After the death of my mum, I didn't understand that grieving was a long process and that one needed to go through it step by step. Initially, I went through guilt that I wasn't there when she passed away. None of my siblings were there with her. They had all gone home that night, planning to return the next day, but by the time they got back to the hospital, it was too late.

I was angry with everyone around me. I felt I'd had enough of carrying everyone's burdens. I became short-tempered, which created unpleasant situations that made me react more negatively, and the vicious circle continued.

I started having palpitations and I was scared. They were a wake-up call for me. I knew if I didn't stop my negative habits, I could end up seriously ill. It was very difficult to change, but I prayed to God for help.

From then on, anytime someone said or did anything that could trigger my anger, I walked away and read a verse of scripture. It wasn't because I suddenly became a saint; it was because I was afraid of the palpitations that would come straight after I had an angry outburst. I learnt how to take deep breaths and refocus on good things. I learnt the true meaning of forgiveness and how to release negative events in the past from my thoughts.

With prayer, I overcame the habit, and the sudden palpitation attacks stopped, but I still experienced lingering ones that were less intense. I was, however, determined to find a solution to these. Needless to say, at that time I was still grieving and didn't know how to deal with my loss.

I am sharing these personal stories with you to make a point: that there is always a pathway to ill health, but with prayer we can find the way out of that. We don't need to become totally dependent on drugs to see us through each day. Toriola, please know that I am not against medication. As you know, I am married to a medical doctor. However, you don't have to depend on drugs forever. There is a better way; you just need to dig deeper, get to the root of the issues that are plaguing you and turn things around for yourself. You have the power and authority to do so because the Spirit of God lives in you.

When I prayed, I received wisdom about how the foundations of fear and anxiety were firmly laid in my early years. I also began to understand the root cause of my anger and how to overcome negative emotions. However, one thing remained: grief.

How does one get over the shock of sudden death in the family? My mother was herself and still walking around when I took her for a check-up at the hospital on a Monday, but by Wednesday her condition had deteriorated, and she died on the Thursday of the same week. I felt numb for many months. I couldn't even cry; I just had a heavy lump in my throat that dropped trickles of water down my throat – maybe those were the tears that should have come out, I don't know. All I know is that my eyes were dry. I was too overwhelmed with grief, disappointment and anger to cry properly.

Despite my grief, I carried on as a wife, mother, teacher and ministry leader. The roles have their challenges, but I continued nonetheless – until my physical symptoms drove me to seek medical help. When, after several tests, the doctors couldn't get to the root of my problems, I decided to empty my emotion tank and retrain my brain to focus on positive thoughts, instead of the difficult things that had happened to me over the years. Some neuroscientists say it takes 21 days for a habit to form, so I knew it wasn't going to be a quick process, but a slow and steady journey. I continued to pray and speak words of encouragement to myself.

It was a big struggle to fight bad thoughts, but gradually, as the days went by, I began to win the battle. I forgave anyone and everyone, and I even made restitution in some cases. I wished everyone well and prayed for those who had hurt me.

The first miracle was that I began to see healing in my relationships. I smiled more and felt at ease. Anyone would think I was on a 'magic pill'. As I emptied emotional toxins, I became lighter and fitter. This lesson will stay with me forever.

My dear Toriola, as you can see, my initiation into peri-menopause was traumatic, and my journey through it was neither linear nor smooth.

I'm sorry that this letter has been very gloomy, but it is important that you know I have been where you are now. This can give you hope that you are not alone on this journey. It will also help you appreciate the positive story of my breakthrough when I share it with you.

I look forward to writing to you again.

Keep healthy and happy.

Much love,

Wura xx

May 2013

Dear Toriola,

I am writing to you from London. I'm here with my daughter Ade to shop for her prom dress. Thanks to the Americans, proms have become a big deal! Anyway, we've bought the dress, and we've ordered her shoes, as we couldn't find her size in the style she wanted. We are all looking forward to her limo trip to Cornwall in July. I was looking at pictures of her as a newborn last night and can hardly believe my daughter is 16; how time flies!

Anyway, enough about us. I got your reply just before I came to London and I am writing to answer your main question about how I found the pathway to healing. I remember you asked this same question months ago, when we communicated by email, but I thought it was best to explain what perimenopause is before I shared my healing story.

In your letter, you said you're always tired and that it seems your prayers are not answered. I want to encourage you to rekindle the flame of hope; it will lead you to your desired breakthrough.

Late last year, when we moved the hands of the clock back by an hour, a thought came to me about time. Calendars and timepieces give us an awareness of dates, years, months, hours, minutes and seconds, but sometimes when I think of eternity,

I ask myself, do I really understand time? Is it linear? When I desperately need a miracle or I'm praying for something, does time, the way I understand it, govern the physical manifestation of what I wish for?

Answers to prayers come in different ways, and sometimes we may not recognise them because they don't show up in the way or form we are expecting. That's why some people say they don't believe in miracles and that prayer is not effective. At one point I almost gave up too, because it seemed heaven was made of 'brass' and my prayers were just bouncing back at me.

Thank God for hope. I decided to restructure my prayers and ask for wisdom on how to get to the root of my affliction, instead of grumbling and recounting all my symptoms to God, as if He didn't already know about them. A few weeks after I made that decision, something happened that challenged what I knew about perimenopause and menopause. That incident, no matter how insignificant it may seem to someone who has never walked the same pathway as me, was the start of my breakthrough, because it rekindled the flame of hope in my heart.

Here's the story:

One day, a friend invited me to work with students at her school in London. The journey was about three hours by train from where we live. She asked me to work there for two days, and my programme was divided into two parts, so I was able to teach creative writing and storytelling.

My friend asked if I wouldn't mind staying at her house, instead of a hotel, and I agreed. On the first night, after work, we went out for a meal, and she noticed I was sweating profusely and looking very tired. When we got back to her house, she asked why I looked so drained, and I told her about my issues. I was so happy she had asked and was eager to share my experiences with her, thinking we would start to compare notes about our hot flushes. However, to my amazement, she said she had never experienced any perimenopause symptoms. She was 58 years old!

I told her she was very lucky to have escaped the horrors of perimenopause, but she was quick to tell me it wasn't luck. She said, 'I made up my mind that I was NOT going to have the symptoms. I declared that those symptoms were not for me; I didn't care about genes or whatever, I wasn't having any of it. Then I refused to think about it'.

Well, that got my attention, but it also got me confused. How can anyone make up her mind not to go through a 'natural' process? I wanted to know more, but her explanations did not make sense to me. They didn't match what I knew about perimenopause. However, I was determined to keep an open mind because at that point I needed a breakthrough.

My friend told me that when she was younger, she heard her aunties and their friends tell their menopause stories. My friend decided that when she got to that season of her life, she wasn't going to tell a similar story and that her own story would be different. According to her, she never expected perimenopause symptoms and she never experienced them. Her period just stopped one day with no associated hot flushes or any other problem.

I didn't know what to do with her story, even though I believe in God and I have faith that all things are possible. My friend's narrative was a very different scenario from praying for someone who was ill to get better. When I started my research into perimenopause symptoms, I found that for most women, these problems were inevitable. So my friend's story was somewhat strange. I did not challenge her or try to poke holes in her narrative; I was simply curious.

I believe my curiosity opened a neural pathway in my brain and created a thought: if my friend could decide not to experience what many people think are natural symptoms, then I could decide to be set free from my health challenges. Slowly but surely, a ray of hope began to shine through my dark alley. I felt encouraged for the first time in months.

The trip to my friend's school had been divinely ordained; it was not mere coincidence. My focus changed, and I stopped seeing myself as a victim of perimenopause symptoms. I understood that my healing was already paid for. In his prophecy about the passion of Christ, Isaiah said: 'But he was pierced for our transgressions, he was crushed for our iniquities; the punishment that brought us peace was on him, and by his wounds we are healed' (Isaiah 53:5). My healing journey started with that ray of hope.

My dear friend, I don't think our recent correspondence is just a coincidence; it could be the answer to your prayers. See it as an opportunity to communicate with someone who has fought and won the battle against the unnatural perimenopause, and who can hold your hand and lead you through it. I know there's a lot that you're struggling with emotionally and physically, but please hang in there. Please don't give up. Have hope.

I look forward to writing to you again when I get back home.

Much love,

Wura xx

June 2013

Dear Toriola,

How's Lagos? I'm sure the rains have come in full force. We are having a lovely summer here. As you know, there are no rainy or dry seasons in England, we have rain all year round, but the summer this year has been absolutely fantastic so far. The Met Office said it is the ninth warmest summer since records began in 1910! To be honest, I think I've acclimatised to the British weather, because I'm feeling the heat, believe it or not.

My husband and the boys are away in London. I called them tonight, and they seem to be enjoying the trip. Ade didn't go with them. She said she needed to rest, as she's just finished her exams. I don't blame her; she worked so hard, bless her.

Has Maria finished her exams? What are your plans for the summer? Ade and I are going to Italy after her prom. I wish we could meet up with you there, but I know you would need to plan such a holiday well in advance. It would be great to see you soon, though; I've missed you terribly!

Ade and I watched *Ratatouille* for the umpteenth time this evening. It was on TV tonight and we couldn't resist watching the classic film again. Amazing story. I can send the DVD version to you in Nigeria if you wish.

The main character in *Ratatouille* is a mouse, and that reminded me of a story I shared with a group last month during one of my storytelling performances. It illustrates what I learnt about hope and I'd like to share it with you.

Story: The two mice

Once upon a time, two mice, Mini and Missy, were playing happily in a farmyard. It was a brilliant, sunny afternoon and all was quiet. The farmer had gone out to fetch some wood for the stove and his wife was sleeping happily on the porch bench.

Suddenly, the mice heard the farmer shouting: 'Get out of here, you vermin! I've just scrubbed that floor and you dirty mice have turned it into your playground. Shoo… shoo… off with you'!

The farmer chased the mice with a broom, and he laughed loudly when he saw that they were trapped; he had pushed them to the edge of the patio. The frightened mice looked at each other helplessly.

'Mini, jump or we'll be squashed by the broom,' Missy cried.

Mini looked down below, saw a large bucket of fresh milk and yelled, 'Do you see that? We'll fall into that bucket of milk and die'!

As the farmer was about to hit them with his broom, Missy grabbed Mini's paw and they jumped. At once, both mice began to swim frantically in the milk.

'Now how do we get out of this horrible mess'? Mini complained bitterly.

'Keep swimming. As long as there's life, there's hope'.

'What hope? You don't expect that someone will come along and save us, do you? I can just see the owner of this bucket singing and dancing for joy at the sight of "vermin" in his milk'! Mini responded.

After many hours of swimming, the mice became tired. Mini's breathing became shallow and he began to sink.

'Hold on, Mini, just keep your head above the milk. Hang in there, my friend'.

'Leave me alone. I can't do this anymore'! Mini cried, and he sank.

Missy was distraught. As night fell, she grieved for her beloved friend, but she kept on splashing around. Eventually, Missy began to find it difficult to swim. It was as if her paws had become heavy and stiff. However, she kept on trying to swim.

The following day, just as the sun was rising on the horizon, Missy looked at her feet and saw that she was standing on a solid mass. She realised that she had churned the milk into butter by swimming around in it. She stepped onto the edge of the bucket, jumped down and made her way home to have a well-deserved rest.

My dear Toriola, have you ever considered why hope is so powerful? It is like an anchor that keeps a ship from drifting back into the sea; hope keeps us stable when a storm rages. When the situation around us yells at us to give up, hope whispers gently, 'Keep going'.

In a previous letter, I told you about a trip to my friend's school and how the discussion I had with her gave me hope. What happened next was that I was able to meditate with a clear mind. Before then, I had chanted verse upon verse from scripture, but my prayers were motivated by fear. No wonder heaven felt like brass.

Unfortunately, the symptoms I had did not disappear

because of my change of focus, and my journey to the final breakthrough was slow. It was frustrating at the time, but hope is a powerful force; it lifts your spirit and makes you want to live again, even if you haven't experienced the breakthrough you are seeking.

My body still ached with pain, and I was plagued by dizzy spells and hot flushes, but I had hope. I was expecting a miracle, so I became more sensitive to the Spirit of God. When Jesus was on earth, he did not heal everyone in the same way. He spoke a word to one, spat on the eye of another to heal him of blindness, and took another man to the outskirts of his village before he healed him. On another occasion, he visited a man called Zacchaeus, who had climbed a tree so that he could see him. Jesus healed him emotionally. Perhaps for me, God needed to deal with what was standing in the way of my healing.

As I prayed, it dawned on me that I had to go back to basics and have faith again. I was ready to make that change. I cried out to God for deliverance, and the words of the prophet Jeremiah became 'living words' in my heart: 'Call to Me and I will answer you, and I will tell you great and mighty things, which you do not know' (33:3).

The 'great and mighty things' came in the form of eight lessons that I learnt as I waded through the unnatural perimenopause. These lessons helped me to find my way out of the dark alley of oppression. They guided me to a total breakthrough, and I became well. Every symptom disappeared, and I knew I had a story to tell. I hope these eight lessons, which I will share with you soon, will encourage you to walk this path so that you too can enjoy abundant health and vitality.

I promise to continue writing to you each month, and I pray that you will find your own pathway to health and wellbeing because you deserve to be happy.

Much love,

Wura xx

July 2013

Dear Toriola,

Greetings from Italy!

I hope you're enjoying your annual leave. My husband and the boys are still away; they are now at Wimbledon. They've just sent me a message to say that Andy Murray won! My husband said Andy won because he and the boys were there to cheer him on. I told him Andy Murray is a tennis genius, ha ha ha!

Ade and I arrived safely in Italy. Neither of us wanted to go with the boys to Wimbledon, so Italy was a great option for us. Our hotel is quite central and close to some historical sites, so we decided to walk to most of the places. It has been a great bonding time for us, and good exercise too.

Yesterday we visited the Pantheon, a former Roman temple which was the largest concrete structure in the world until the 20th century. The magic starts when you step inside the humongous building – great artefacts and history! From there we went to the Fontana di Trevi, the biggest fountain in the world. I saw some people dropping coins into the water and making wishes. It was heart-warming to see this in our modern world of technological advancement.

Of all the places we have visited, I had the most humbling experience at the Mamertine Prison, where Paul the Apostle was incarcerated. The bare floor and tiny cell made me stand in awe of the great apostle, as I reflected on the price he paid to spread the gospel that we are enjoying today.

We are planning to visit the Colosseum tomorrow. I am sure that will be the experience of a lifetime! I have wanted to visit Rome since my first year as a Classics student at the University of Ibadan, so this really is a dream come true.

I forgot to mention in my last letter that I got my certification as a health coach and nutrition advisor! I started the training about two years ago. I was curious to know more about the role of nutrition in health and wellbeing, so I enrolled as a part-time student. I have now finished the first stage.

I'm so happy to hear that you've joined a health club in Lagos. Please make sure you go regularly; I think it is a good investment in your health.

In a previous letter, I explained some of the factors that may contribute to unnatural perimenopause. These can include stress, an unhealthy lifestyle, viruses and a sluggish liver that underperforms in its function to cleanse the body and rid it of toxins and pathogens.

You said in your last letter that you'd found some information about toxicity and would like to know more, so I'm going to address that. It is a topic that I really enjoy teaching now; hopefully, it will be clearer to you after you've read this letter.

First, I'd like to start with a story.

Story: The petrol tank

A mother of two young children decided to restart her mobile-hairdressing business after her husband lost his job. She posted leaflets wherever she could and waited for someone to call. She waited six weeks before a woman called to book an appointment. The hairdresser was excited, and she prepared for her first booking.

The client's house was ten miles away, and on the way there the hairdresser realised there was not enough fuel in her car, so she stopped at a nearby petrol station. As she put the nozzle back in its holder, she realised she had filled her car with diesel instead of petrol. *Oh well, I'll use this up and fill it with petrol another time,* she thought.

Soon she was on her way, but the car began to give out smoke. The sound coming from it was like someone with a bad case of hiccups. The noise gradually increased, until the car spluttered to a stop right in front of a traffic light, miles away from her destination.

As the hairdresser jumped out of the car, a man who had noticed the smoke walked up to her.

'What's the problem, madam'?

The hairdresser looked up, alarmed. 'I don't know. I… I… Well, first it began smoking, and then bang, bang, bang'.

The man, who was a mechanic, opened the bonnet. 'Have you just put fuel in this car?'

'Yes. I mistakenly filled it with diesel – my car runs on petrol'.

The mechanic shook his head. 'That explains things. You really shouldn't have driven the car when you realised your mistake'.

The woman was upset. 'Can you just help me get it back on the road, please?' she asked. 'I really have to get to my client in a few minutes'.

'I'm sorry, madam, but every drop of diesel must be

drained and the tank must be thoroughly cleaned. Then, if you're lucky and the car isn't damaged, you'll be able to get it back on the road'.

The hairdresser thanked the man and called the AA. Soon they arrived and set to work on the vehicle.

This story encapsulates what I'm about to share with you; it was the first significant lesson I learnt on my journey through the unnatural perimenopause.

Lesson 1: The negative effects of toxins on the body

The root of most illnesses, diseases and many symptoms associated with the unnatural perimenopause can be attributed to toxicity, but where do toxins come from?

External sources

We are exposed to toxins daily. They are in our food, toothpaste, bath soap, shampoo and the air we breathe. Even the water we drink is overloaded with purifying chemicals. Food laden with toxins such as pesticides, poor diets and unhealthy lifestyles put a lot of stress on the body. Though the body does an excellent job of fighting these noxious enemies, there are times when it is just too overloaded to do the job.

The effects of these toxins can be likened to the experience of the hairdresser whose car stopped functioning when she filled it with the wrong fuel.

Internal sources

The human body is constantly attacked internally by reactive particles known as free radicals. These are formed when weak bonds break apart. However, the radicals really do not want to be free, because they are unstable; they need another molecule to pair with. So they go around looking for a stable molecule in order to take its electron. In the process, they can damage other living cells and even alter their DNA. The good news is that the body has natural antioxidants to fight free radicals. However, when the body is weak, it may lack these crucial neutralisers and illness may set in.

It is important to note that free radicals are not entirely bad news; some are beneficial to the body. One such free radical is hydrogen peroxide. White blood cells use hydrogen peroxide to kill cancer cells and pathogens. Balance is crucial when it comes to antioxidants and free radicals in the body. It is essential that the body produces enough antioxidants to neutralise the activities of free radicals so that they are kept to the necessary minimum, or the body will experience trauma.

Our amazing self-healing bodies can be re-energised and boosted to start functioning well again. The body comprises trillions of cells that work tirelessly to absorb nutrients and remove waste. These cells die and get replaced through a process called mitosis. The best way to get the body to produce healthy cells is by feeding it what it needs most - great nutrients found in living foods that are rich in antioxidants. By living foods, I mean fresh, vibrant, unprocessed foods. Healthy cells that function optimally give us the energy to get up in the morning, go to work, exercise, sleep well and enjoy life.

Once I understood this information, I began to give my body superior materials with which to build healthy new cells. My allergies, intolerances and perimenopause symptoms then eased.

I learnt that to get rid of a health problem, I needed to go to the root of the issue and eliminate it. Some people need medical intervention to stabilise them, but drugs are really not the solution to many health issues. If they were, people would not be on them perpetually. Getting to the root of illnesses is better than masking them with drugs because many drugs have negative side effects.

Once you've taken that initial step, the next thing to do is find a natural healing pathway. That was what I did. At the age of 46, while dealing with perimenopause symptoms, I embarked on a detoxification journey, and the results were amazing. Why did I leave it until I was 46? Here's the simple answer: I was ignorant. No one had taught me what my body needed to function optimally.

My dear, I hope this letter has given you clarity on the topic of toxicity. I look forward to sharing more information with you soon.

Much love,

Wura xx

August 2013

Dear Toriola,

Ade and I are back home. Italy was great; we had a blissful time. There was a lot to see and do, and the weather was good, but it was too warm for me. The highlight of the trip was the U Fistinu of Saint Rosalia, a big festival in Palermo. We danced to our hearts' content as we joined the procession around the 50-foot float. The music was out of this world, and as for the food… I have no words to describe it. My favourite was panna cotta, a classic Italian dessert made with cream.

A few years ago, when I first discovered panna cotta in England, I couldn't eat it because I was intolerant to lactose and couldn't eat any form of dairy or egg. I later discovered that the intolerance was because of issues in my gut. I will share the story of how I was healed later, but I wanted you to know why I was so thankful that I could eat food made with a dairy product. As I took each spoonful of vanilla-infused Italian panna cotta, I gave thanks for another opportunity to eat anything I liked! Panna cotta is not on my list of healthy meals, but while on holiday I welcomed the chance to taste the rich dessert.

I am excited to hear that your health is improving. Great news! I'm flattered that you are using my letters 'as a health guide'. Please stop saying thank you in every reply you send me – what are friends for? I am just happy that you find my letters helpful. I believe that sometime soon you will also share the story of your journey from illness to health and I will be there to rejoice with you.

Today, I want to explore Lesson 2 with you, because in your last letter you requested that I tell you the specific things I did to help me get rid of toxins. As you know, each person is unique. What is useful for one person may not be beneficial to another, even if they are experiencing the same symptoms. Nevertheless, I am happy to share my experiences with you.

Lesson 2: Deep-cleansing process

When the body is overwhelmed by internal and external attacks, one way of addressing the issue is to give the liver some tender loving care.

The liver is a very powerful organ, and many health issues that we experience in today's world stem from this organ malfunctioning. The liver is the protector of the human being. It cleans up after us, works extra hard to keep us whole, and stores the necessary minerals and vitamins that the body needs to function. Imagine this machine being overburdened with toxins from both internal and external sources! The result is a weak body with a weak immune system. All hell could break loose.

For many months at the start of my healing journey, I focused on getting my gut healthy. However, I began to study the functions of the liver and how toxins create chaos, and I turned my attention to caring for my powerhouse – the liver. Whole, organic, plant-based foods can help to nurture the body, rid it of toxins and build healthy cells. As you feed your body the foods it needs to function properly, the toxins that your body has hidden away are flushed out. The intelligence of our self-healing and self-cleansing body is amazing!

Toriola, in your letter you asked that I give you specific details on what I did daily when I started my health and wellbeing journey. Firstly, I went through a chelation process (more on this below) with the help of a health coach. Then we put together a daily routine, which I refer to as maintenance.

I will share with you my daily routine in a moment - first, a note on what to expect when the toxins leave your body.

Detoxifying safely

There are several ways toxins can be eliminated from the body: through the mucous membrane, the skin and bowel movements. A negative effect of detoxification is toxin elimination. Some people have bad sinusitis, itching and constant headaches, and some move their bowels more often than normal.

Sometimes, these symptoms can be intense. Hence, it is best to work with a knowledgeable practitioner who can guide you through the process. Many health practitioners offer chelation services; they provide herbs and medicines that bind with toxins and direct them through a proper elimination channel, rather than the toxins being left to float around the body.

It is essential to go and see your doctor to get a diagnosis whenever you experience any symptom that concerns you. I think it is also a good idea to work with a health coach who can guide you on how to eliminate toxins from your body safely.

Now, I will share with you how I cleanse my body and strengthen my immune system.

Step 1: Oil pulling
I start my cleansing journey in the mouth because it is the gateway to the body and the entry point to the digestive system. Various types of bacteria inhabit the tongue and mouth, some of which can be harmful if they find their way further into the body.

Oil pulling is an ancient method by which you can pull these bacteria out. I take a teaspoon of organic, cold-pressed coconut oil and swish it around in my mouth, pushing it through the teeth, for 15 to 20 minutes. Then I spit it out into a small bin bag, so it doesn't clog my sink. You must NOT swallow the oil under any circumstances. When I finish, I rinse my mouth thoroughly with water and then brush my teeth with non-fluoride toothpaste.

It is easy to make this a part of your daily routine. I sometimes do it twice a day, in the morning before brushing my teeth, and at night just before I go to bed. Initially, I found it boring just sitting and swishing, but now I read a book, watch an interesting video or check my emails while doing oil pulling.

Many people have testified to the healing effects of this ancient practice. Some say it got rid of their sinusitis, for example, and others say they were able to sleep better. When I started oil pulling, I noticed that my sinus problem was worse on the first day; however, this only lasted for 24 hours. Within a few days, my body was rid of the troublesome sinusitis that had plagued my life since my teenage years. I felt much better, and the bonus was that I no longer had a persistent bleeding gum problem either.

Some people react negatively to oil pulling initially, but they soon feel better and can continue. One of my clients, a woman who was on my weight-loss programme, started oil pulling on the first day of her detox programme, but she had terrible nausea and had to stop until she had completed her juice fast. Immediately after she stopped, she felt better. After her juice fast, she started oil pulling again, and the side effects were not as dramatic. I wasn't surprised by the way her body reacted to the oil pulling; it is a powerful method of starting a detox.

Oil pulling with organic coconut oil pulls toxic germs from your oral cavity. It is more effective than most mouthwashes, because of the healing properties of the coconut. I recommend that you read Dr Bruce Fife's book *Oil Pulling Therapy*. The book goes into more detail on this natural healing technique and explains why it works. You'll also find testimonies of numerous people and scientific research about its healing effects.

Step 2: Juice and Smoothie

I once watched a video on YouTube titled 'Fat, Sick and Nearly Dead' and it changed my life. I watched a man cleanse his body of all ailments and weight problems after going on a juice fast for 60 days. Prior to his fast, he had been on countless medications, but by the time he finished the doctors had taken him off all of them. That video was the encouragement I needed, although, I wouldn't encourage someone who has not been eating healthily or whose body is overloaded with toxins to go on a long fast.

After oil pulling, I drink a cup of warm water infused with lemon. I always add lemon to the water because it boosts the body's immunity, as it contains citric acid, magnesium, calcium, vitamin C and limonene. Lemon aids the detoxification process because of the way it stimulates and cleanses the liver. It also addresses some of the problems caused by dehydration.

After about 45 minutes, I drink a glass of green juice, freshly made with my masticating juicer. My green juice usually contains celery, ginger, kale, spinach and cucumber, but the recipe varies daily. If I'm fasting, I will continue to hydrate myself throughout the day by drinking pure filtered water.

Later, I'll have a glass of homemade smoothie. Some of the ingredients I use in my smoothies are strawberries, blueberries, kiwis, cranberries and apples. I may add beetroot, but only about a quarter of a whole beet because it is a potent vegetable that can help to lower blood pressure. (If you have low blood pressure, be very careful with the consumption of beets.) You will notice that this smoothie contains a lot of berries; this is because they are a great source of antioxidants. The aim is to detoxify, and these antioxidants help to rejuvenate my body as it gets rid of toxins. They also protect the body from damaging free radicals.

I add two tablespoons of organic shelled hemp seed and two tablespoons of chia seed to my smoothie. Hemp seed provides up to 50 percent of the body's recommended daily allowance of magnesium, a mineral that many people lack, and about 25 percent of zinc, which is great for healing the gut.

If I'm not fasting, I eat a healthy lunch and dinner. However, if I'm fasting, I eat a bowl of nourishing salad and drink a glass of water in the evening. Some people break their fast with another glass of smoothie or juice, but I prefer a light meal.

I sometimes embark on a three-day juice fast, after which I feel rejuvenated because my digestive system has had a rest from continuously being clogged by cooked meals. One advantage of doing a juice fast (although I do not advocate doing it for the long term) is that it strengthens the immune system. When that happens, the body is able to heal faster.

When I'm not on a fast, I juice plain celery without adding any other vegetable. I usually aim for about sixteen ounces. Celery is a powerful medicine whose cluster salts bind to pathogens and neurotoxins and eliminate them from the body. It supports the immune system as it works tirelessly to kill bacteria and viruses. It also helps to increase hydrochloric acid and keeps blood pressure balanced. Researcher and holistic coach, Anthony Williams provides great information on the power of this humble vegetable; please check online for more information.

Vitamins and herbs are powerful

Some that I use regularly, which I purchase from reputable organic sellers, include: Vitamin B12, vitamin D3 with K2, Zinc, lemon balm, cat's claws, spirulina and nettle leaf. I follow the manufacturers' instructions and add these to smoothies or water. These herbs are known to strengthen the liver and also attack the dreaded Epstein Barr virus. When the immune system is strengthened, the body functions optimally.

The result of strengthening the immune system

'You are what you eat' is a popular saying. I would add, 'You are what your body absorbs'. One day, I went for a blood test at my GP's surgery, and the results showed that I was iron deficient, and my haemoglobin was very low. The doctor was baffled because for some reason my body was not absorbing iron. No one had told me then about gut health, toxicity or deficiencies. The doctor placed me on yet another course of iron tablets. On that occasion, the prescription read 'Take these three times a day'. At that point, I knew if I kept taking those tablets, I could eventually suffer liver damage.

My doctor was not getting to the root of the problem, but I was determined to do so. I began to research why my body was not absorbing the nutrients it needed, and I found that I could not simply continue to 'pour new wine into an old skin bottle' – I needed to cleanse my liver. My unending vertigo, dizziness and head pressure were partly due to my low haemoglobin, and they had become compounded when I hit perimenopause.

Toriola, I'm sure by now you're eager to know what happened after I embarked on my healthy lifestyle. Well, I slowly began to feel better and happier. My body was absorbing nutrients, and my haemoglobin and iron levels went back to normal. The greatest news, however, was that after about ten years of food allergies, I was healed and was able to eat egg, yoghurt, cake and chocolate again. I'll share that story with you in my next letter. Although I don't intend to make eating loads of dairy products, including chocolate, a habit, at least I can eat what I want, and if I don't, it is my choice.

My dear, I hope this letter is helpful. I look forward to hearing from you.

Be blessed, my friend.

Much love,

Wura xx

September 2013

Dear Toriola,

I got your letter yesterday and I couldn't wait to send you a reply because you sounded so excited about the information I sent you on detoxification. I didn't realise you are lactose intolerant. Yes, I remember the restaurant we went to in Ibadan when we were planning my mum's funeral. The waitress asked if we wanted dessert and both of us declined. I couldn't eat it because of my intolerance to dairy at that time, but I thought you were just watching your weight.

You're right, it is dreadful, but it isn't just because Africans cannot tolerate milk; many Caucasians are also intolerant to lactose. Having said that, I now know that what many people self-diagnose as lactose intolerance could be what health practitioners call leaky gut, or it could be the effects of having a low level of hydrochloric acid in the stomach.

Since you're very keen to know more, I will explain some of the problems that arise when the gut is not healthy, in Lesson 3 below. A healthy gut enables the body to absorb nutrients from the food we eat. If the gut is unhealthy, we become deficient in essential nutrients. The body then struggles to function optimally, and this could lead to some of the issues that present as symptoms of unnatural perimenopause.

Lesson 3: Deficiency

Toxicity and deficiency are two major causes of illnesses, diseases and malfunctioning of the systems in the body. Such malfunctions can cause the symptoms of unnatural perimenopause.

I don't have the statistics for Nigeria, but in the UK about 25 million people suffer from digestive issues; that's about a third of the population. Unfortunately, issues with the digestive system can be the foundation for other health issues. This is because over 70 percent of our immune system is in the gut and a huge percentage of the body's serotonin is produced in the gut. If there is a problem in this area, the body may not be able to absorb the nutrients it needs to build healthy new cells. This leaves the body deficient of what it needs to function optimally.

What's your gut feeling?

Balanced and healthy gut flora could save your life. An imbalance of microflora, known as dysbiosis, could cause problems for the digestive system. Such imbalances have several causes, such as the use of antibiotics, stress, traumatic experiences and, importantly, low production of hydrochloric acid (HCL). This acid helps to break down foods in the stomach and contributes to protein digestion. When food is well digested, it does not rot away or cling to the walls of the gastrointestinal tract (GI tract). HCL also helps to destroy the toxins in the food that enter the digestive system, so a lack of or inadequate secretion of HCL could be lethal.

Another function of hydrochloric acid is to help prevent infection by killing pathogens in the stomach. When there is a deficiency of this important acid, toxins and bad bacteria could enter the intestines unchecked, thus creating an imbalance of gut flora. When the digestive system is exposed to toxins, the villi walls are enlarged, and undigested food and toxins freely enter the bloodstream, leading to various food intolerances.

HCL also helps the body to absorb vitamin B12, which I call 'the happy vitamin'. A deficiency of this vitamin can cause many of the symptoms associated with perimenopause, including mild depression, ringing in the ears, a tingling sensation in the hands and feet, anaemia and fatigue. Vitamin B12 helps build the red blood cells that carry oxygen around the body, hence some people feel tired when the body does not have enough of this vitamin.

My dear, you can see why the gut is a 'powerhouse' and how the entire body is at risk when it is malfunctioning. If the body is not able to absorb nutrients from food, it cannot function optimally. When I learnt this lesson, I took the next step and began to deal with deficiencies. How can you do this successfully?

Pay attention to your eating habits

The first thing I did once I understood the importance of proper food digestion was to pay attention to my eating habits. Digestion of food starts before you put food in your mouth. We salivate when we smell food because the salivary amylase is released in readiness for digestion. It is therefore crucial to treat each mealtime as important.

I have stopped rushing around while eating; I sit down, relax and enjoy my meal. This helps maximise the secretion of stomach acid, which aids digestion.

I chew each mouthful properly. This allows my food to be well digested. When food is not chewed well, the partially digested food could ferment and putrefy in the lining of the intestine, instead of moving effortlessly through. This could cause bloating and pain.

Increase hydrochloric acid

One very efficient way of increasing hydrochloric acid, which is essential for breaking down protein, is by juicing organic celery every morning and drinking it on an empty stomach. You can start with 8 ounces and gradually build up to 16 ounces. Celery contains alkalising elements (sodium, magnesium, potassium and calcium), and it rebuilds and increases depleted hydrochloric acid. Sometimes I also add the juice of half a lemon to a glass of water and drink that 30 minutes before a meal.

After several weeks of this routine, I noticed that I no longer experienced bloating, cramps and acid reflux after certain meals, because I was digesting my food properly.

Repair the damage

Many years ago, when I was living in Nigeria, I saw a man trying to repair a damaged table made of iron. One of the legs was broken and the man replaced it with a piece of wood. Needless to say, it was not a job well done; the finished product was ugly and ineffective, and the table kept tipping over.

Recently, while on my healing journey, that image came to my mind. When you want to repair something, you need to fix it with the appropriate material. You can't repair a table made of iron with wood and expect to get a good result. Perhaps it'll be steady for a while, but it'll soon fall apart. We can apply this same principle to our bodies.

When the body has broken down because of deficiencies, you must find the appropriate materials to rebuild it. To know what the body needs, let's revisit the creation story to see how the human body was formed. According to the book of Genesis, when God was about to create the earth, He spoke words and things came into existence: light, water, land and other things. However, when He was going to create the human being, He spoke words – 'Let us make man in our image' – but He did not stop there. He rolled up His sleeves... 'then the Lord God formed the man of dust from the ground'.

Numerous elements found in soil are also found in the human body – oxygen, carbon, nitrogen, iron, calcium and potassium, to name but a few. It therefore makes sense that when the body is not functioning optimally, it is best to repair it with the materials from which it was made. According to the creation story, soil was the building material for the body. So the best place to find these essential nutrients is whole, organic foods in their natural forms.

The body needs the essential nutrients, phytonutrients and minerals found in whole, organic foods to help it get rid of free radicals. These nutrients also rejuvenate the body. Today, I feel more energetic than I did in my 20s. I sprint up the stairs without even thinking about it. That was almost impossible before my cleansing programme. In my last letter, I told you about the juice fast that I did when I learnt about toxicity. That knowledge, in addition to the lesson I learnt about deficiencies and how to pay attention to my eating habits, gave me an insight into how the body can be rejuvenated.

Over time, my gut healed. It was like a miracle. I was able to eat egg, yoghurt and cheese again – things I had been unable to consume for ten years! About six months after my first juice fast, I went to my GP to have another blood test. The results showed that my iron levels, which used to be dangerously low, were back to normal, and they have stayed normal ever since.

I'll share with you some more of the things that helped me to heal my gut.

Probiotics

This means 'for life'. They are friendly bacteria that help the immune system to function optimally by controlling the growth of harmful bacteria. Some of the recognised types of healthy bacteria are: bifidobacteria, lactobacilli and bacillus subtilis. 'Probiotics' is also a general name for live microbial supplements that help to enhance the balance of gut flora.

With my newly found knowledge about how to keep my digestive system healthy, I decided to include probiotics in my diet. To have the desired effect, a probiotic supplement must be delivered live into the gut and survive the strong acidic environment of the stomach, especially when taken first thing in the morning before food. It should thrive in the intestines and targeted areas of the gut and should start to work immediately. Unfortunately, many probiotic supplements have a limited shelf life, and some cannot survive the harsh acidic conditions of the stomach, which makes elevated biotics or prebiotics better options for the digestive system.

Elevated biotics

Anthony Williams, a holistic health practitioner, describes elevated biotics as microscopic, life-giving organisms that cover or sit on leaves and the skins of raw organic produce that is unwashed or rinsed lightly. Elevated biotics survive the digestive process and make it to the ileum, where they create vitamin B12.

To get a good source of elevated biotics, I started growing kale, strawberries and broccoli in my back garden. When I harvest them, I munch on a handful without rinsing it, because I know I grew the produce organically.

Toriola, I know planting your produce may be challenging, as you live in a block of flats in a big city, but you can find a trusted, local organic farm, visit them and find out about their planting practices. You can then buy some of their produce and eat it raw after you've rinsed it lightly.

Prebiotics

Prebiotics are non-digestible complex carbohydrates; hence they can arrive in the colon intact. They benefit friendly bacteria by stimulating their growth and improving their health, and they also curtail the activities of bad bacteria. Dr Paul Clayton, a nutrition scientist, says that when the good bacteria multiply, they secrete enzymes that break down prebiotics to acetic and butyric acid. These acids restrict the growth of bad bacteria. Simply put, prebiotics are food for the good bacteria and they make them flourish. Foods that are rich in prebiotics include: dandelion greens, apple, asparagus, Jerusalem artichoke, onion, banana, garlic, cabbage and leek.

I believe that my daily routine of juicing a variety of complex carbohydrates may have helped to enhance my microbial balance. Indeed, 'when you know the truth it shall set you free'. I was set free from symptoms of food intolerance that had plagued me for ten years. When my gut was healed, my body began to absorb nutrients from the food I ate, and I became stronger, healthier and happier.

The bonus to my cleansing and detoxification was weight loss. For about thirteen years, I had tried to lose weight on yoyo diets. Then, within twelve months of embarking on a healthy lifestyle journey, I'd lost ten kilograms. I didn't set out to lose weight, but I welcomed my new look with excitement. The only problem was that I had to change my wardrobe because my old clothes looked terrible on me!

Eliminate the 'whites'

After I repaired the damage in my gut, I gradually eliminated the 'whites' from my diet. One by one, I threw out, 'white' carbohydrates, such as pasta, bread and sugar, and sourced healthier alternatives. I also drastically reduced my portion size of white rice. Within a few weeks, my hot flushes began to dwindle, and I no longer had palpitations.

For many years, I had eaten various processed foods nearly every day and avoided fruits and vegetables. My family would tell a tale about my white rice obsession when I was younger; they called it 'Panadol'. It started one day when I was in secondary school. I was very ill with malaria fever and couldn't eat anything. My dad told my mum, 'Give her rice; it's her Panadol. It is the only thing she'll eat even when she's ill.' Everyone fell about laughing and watched as I ate a bowl of white rice even though I'd vomited up everything else. My obsession with white rice continued for many more years until I hit perimenopause.

I was amazed that just changing my diet and eating healthily had brought me so much relief. Socrates said, 'Let food be thy medicine and medicine be thy food'; those words are so true.

My friend, I know that 'eliminating the whites' may be the most challenging step for you; however, considering the severity of your hot flushes, as you described in your last letter, I think you may benefit from changing your diet in this way.

Beware of gene-altering carcinogens in your food

According to Dr Ann Wigmore in her book *The Wheatgrass Book*, some of the contaminants in our modern diet are 'carcinogenic (cancer-causing) or mutagenic (capable of altering genes or DNA and possibly affecting future generations)'. We may not be able to totally avoid these foods, but we can strengthen our bodies by eating healthily. Scientists have discovered that chlorophyll found in raw leafy vegetables, especially wheatgrass, can protect us from carcinogens, and detoxify the liver.

Another controversial subject is the negative effect of bisphenol A (BPA), which is used for making plastics. It is an endocrine disruptor and has the potential to alter genes. An abundance of synthetic xenoestrogen like this can also trigger perimenopausal symptoms because it can imitate the effects of natural oestrogen and can cause disorders of the reproductive system.

In her article 'The scary new evidence on BPA-free plastics', Mariah Blake explored the conspiracy theories about BPA and the so-called BPA-free plastics. She refers to research findings that show that BPA can switch off a gene. Blake also refers to the findings of Frederick vom Saal, a Missouri University biologist who says, 'A poison kills you; a chemical like BPA reprograms your cells and ends up causing a disease in your grandchild that kills him'.

Many years ago, I read an ancient scripture that left me confused: 'choose life, so that you and your descendants may live' (Deuteronomy 30:19). The first time I came across this passage I didn't understand how people's choices could affect their descendants. However, I later discovered that the contaminants in our modern diet and the food available to us in supermarkets could be harmful, as they can alter our genes.

It is interesting how science is now catching up with scripture. Scientific research that shows how our modern food can harm our bodies also suggests that in every generation people make choices that could later affect their descendants. So we need to examine our choices carefully.

I am not sure how you can avoid plastic, but let's put our heads together to find a way. Rather than relying on bottled water, I use a filtering system that uses carbon filtration to purify water. It removes fluoride, which is a brain toxin, lead, arsenic, chlorine and various other pathogens that are harmful to the body. I'll find out if they can ship to Nigeria.

My dear Toriola, when I understood how my body functions and what to do to keep it healthy, I made the decision to neutralise the polluting mutagenic contaminants in my body, and since that time I've seen a dramatic change in my health and wellbeing. Some people would call it a miracle; I call it knowing the truth and being set free. My point here is that we need to know the real enemy that challenges the abundant health that God has made available to us, and we need to eliminate it.

In this letter, I have analysed several ways of dealing with the problem of deficiencies in the body through diet. I hope these make sense to you and that you find the information useful. I look forward to writing to you again.

Be blessed.

Much love,

Wura xx

October 2013

Dear Toriola,

Congrats on your latest news. I'm sure it was an emotional experience seeing Remilekun off to uni, but he'll be fine. I'm not saying it is easy; nevertheless, our prayer as parents is that our children will succeed in whatever they do. How's Maria coping? I hope she's not missing her brother too much.

How is your right knee? Has the swelling gone down? When I got your letter two days ago, I called the new mobile number you sent to me, but I couldn't get through. I wanted to find out how you're doing because you said the pain is bad and that you still have dizzy spells when you get up after sitting for a long time. Calls to Nigeria are expensive and I wouldn't have been able to explain the things in this letter to you over the phone, but it would have been good to hear your voice. I will try that number again soon.

Coincidentally, Lesson 4 is about 'getting up and moving'. You may find it relevant, considering that in your work as a bank manager you sit for long hours at a desk. Not moving around enough may be a contributing factor in your pain and the spinning sensation you feel at times. However, I would advise that you see your doctor as soon as possible. You can also request to see an ENT specialist so that they can carry out tests for vestibular disorders. Your inner ear and brain are parts of the vestibular system, and two of the symptoms of the disorders are imbalance and dizziness.

You also said that you are concerned about arthritis. My answer to your question is, speak to your doctors. They may ask you to go for an X-ray, and that will give you a definite answer. I went through a similar situation a few years ago and I will share my experiences with you.

Lesson 4: Get up and move

A few years ago, I noticed a swelling in my left knee, and the pain was excruciating. My sedentary lifestyle began after Ade started school, about 12 years ago. I didn't have to run around after the kids like I used to when they were toddlers. I focused on my writing and sat for hours in front of the computer. This lifestyle – never exercising, sitting for long hours at my desk, eating in front of the TV and sleeping late – was devastating to my health. I experienced vertigo and lethargy, and I had double vision most days.

My deliverance came when I decided to start walking and exercising. The first few days were terrible. I took a short walk to our corner shop for the first time in many months (previously, I would drive there). As I walked, I soon began to feel terrible itching all over my body. It was so embarrassing that I turned around and hurried back home.

Despite this setback, I was determined to succeed, so I tried again and again – but the same thing happened. I went to the gym, but as soon as I got on the treadmill, the itching began. I cancelled my membership, bought a treadmill to use at home and scratched my way through each exercise in a quiet corner of my study. I complained about the itching to a physician, and he thought it was all in my head, especially after the antihistamine drugs he recommended were ineffective.

A few months later, a friend told me she had experienced the same symptom, but she had continued walking and the itching had stopped. So I kept walking – and after a few weeks, the itching stopped and my knee was back to normal! I was so excited that I kept to my routine and walked around my neighbourhood for about 30 minutes every day.

In her book, *Sitting Kills, Moving Heals*, Dr Joan Vernikos describes one of her experiments with astronauts – a few young crews and an elderly 77-year-old crew. They found that irrespective of age, all the astronauts experienced the same physical degeneration after spending nine days in space. The reason is that there is no gravity in space. When astronauts first return to earth, some have less stamina and they shuffle when they walk because they have lost their sense of balance. The good news is that after a regime of exercises, they soon recover.

The researchers then got a group of healthy young men and women to lie on their backs continually so that they would be in a similar situation to the astronauts in space without gravity. Gravitational pull is reduced when people lie down because gravity does not pull down from head to toe, rather, it pulls across the torso.

The research concluded that the subjects who lay on their back for a long time had similar symptoms of imbalance and shuffling when walking as those who went to space. However, just like the astronauts, they recovered soon after the experiment, when they began to move around.

According to Dr Joan Vernikos, gravity grounds us as we feel its pull when we stand up; hence people feel more comfortable sitting down than getting up. Gravity is the reason why it is easier to run downhill than uphill. The problem is that our modern sedentary lifestyle encourages us to give in to the gravitational pull: we enjoy sitting for long periods in armchairs, staying in bed for longer or taking the lift instead of the stairs. Unfortunately, such a sedentary lifestyle 'wastes' our bones and muscles, and the brain could experience atrophy.

The body is created to be mobile; we must keep moving and use gravity to our advantage. Unfortunately, our modern-day conveniences and gadgets deprive us of this very important aspect of a healthy lifestyle – moving.

The importance of exercising

Exercise helps your body to take in the oxygen that it needs to stay alive. We may be able to survive forty days without food, and maybe three to four days without water, but we cannot survive five minutes without oxygen. It is the breath of life.

Let's talk about the lymphatic system. Its job is to move debris, dumped by the cells, out of the body. Unlike the heart, which can pump blood around the body, the lymphatic system functions through movement. That is why exercise is about much more than keeping fit or building muscles – moving the body is crucial to your wellbeing. The movement doesn't have to be rigorous; regularly spending a few minutes on a rebounder or mini trampoline could work wonders, strengthening the immune system and helping to activate the production of antibodies.

Toriola, I still remember the day you came to my house, back in 2000 when I visited Nigeria, and you met my grandmother. You said she was beautiful and energetic, and you were surprised when I told you she was 90 years old. She died three years after you met her, but throughout her life, she never stepped on a treadmill. She reached to the top shelf to get jars, bent down to grind peppercorns on her stone mill, pounded yam in her mortar, hand-washed her clothes and cooked fresh meals daily. All day she moved from one place to another; you wouldn't see her sitting down for more than ten minutes at a time. She was steady on her feet until her last days.

Two years before she died, I bought her a beautifully crafted walking stick, thinking she might need it at some point. She said thanks, placed it gently in a corner in her room and never touched it again. My grandmother had only been to the hospital twice in her life, when she went to have her two children – my mum and my uncle. One morning, on the longest day of the year in June 2003, she woke up, went to the bathroom and told my mum that she wasn't feeling well. Then she went back to her bed, curled up and passed away. She was 93.

My grandmother had lived in unpleasant circumstances amongst rivals, because her husband, who was much older than her, had other wives. She was the last and youngest wife in a polygamous home. She didn't have much – only a tiny field where she planted crops for her children and a tin-roofed corner shop where she sold groceries. Nevertheless, she had a large heart that accommodated everyone. When I think about my grandmother, I remember the importance of certain things that we need to do daily to get the most out of the beautiful and wonderfully created body that we've been given.

One of the things I did when I learnt this fourth lesson was to go on my treadmill once a day to exercise. However, I continued to sit for long hours at my computer for the rest of the day. Unfortunately, despite my treadmill exercise I didn't get any better, so I intensified my research. That was when I found Dr Vernikos's book *Sitting Kills, Moving Heals*. According to this amazing author, 'exercise is not a substitute for activities that come naturally throughout the day, 365 days a year, for the rest of your life'. It is consistent movement throughout the day that sustains the body.

After learning about the negative effects of a sedentary lifestyle on the body, I changed my habits and engaged in activities that involved getting up every 30 minutes, even when in the middle of a writing project. I did stretching and squatting exercises. I moved, moved more and moved again. Within a few weeks, I began to see positive results.

The first noticeable change was that my balance was restored. Before, each time I got off my comfortable armchair I felt light-headed and unsteady on my feet. However, once I started getting out of my chair every so often, the staggering stopped. The squatting exercises were good for my brain because as I pushed my body down and up again, blood was pumped to my brain. I believe that's the reason why the vertigo that I had experienced occasionally became history.

My hot flushes also reduced considerably, even though they still occurred sporadically. While in the past, sitting for long hours used to make my legs ache, getting up now and again restored my leg muscles, which were beginning to atrophy.

I am sharing this lesson with you because if you understand how your body works and you give it what it needs to survive, you will be walking down the pathway to a joyful life and abundant health.

My dear, you need more than just a few minutes a day on the treadmill. Do not substitute this for activities that you should be doing throughout the day. Moving is easier than it sounds. There are a few things you can incorporate into your daily routine. You may wish to consider the following:

- Tell your driver to stop the car about ten minutes away from your office and walk the rest of the way
- Take the stairs instead of the lift
- Stand up from your desk every 30 minutes and walk around
- At lunch, eat your meal and then go out and take a brisk walk around your office, instead of eating at your desk and then continuing with work straight after
- At the weekend, walk a few miles with a 'walking buddy', or do it alone. I find it easier when I walk with a friend because it helps us to be accountable to each other

Creativity is key when it comes to getting up and moving.

I look forward to writing to you soon. In the meantime, keep moving!

Much love,

Wura xx

November 2013

Dear Toriola,

It was great to hear your voice again on the phone, after such a long time! How is Remilekun? I hope he's settling in well at uni. How's my darling Maria? She sent me a message on Facebook yesterday, saying she would love to come and spend her next summer holiday with us. I think it's a brilliant idea. Ade said she couldn't wait to see her. I think they're getting on well; I saw Ade chatting with her on WhatsApp last week. I'm delighted with their friendship.

Thanks for updating me about the health club. What you said about the aerobics class that you recently joined was funny. However, I don't think you should give up just because you're finding it difficult to synchronise with the others. You said the class started in August, which means they've been dancing for about three months before you joined them. Speak with the instructor and see if she will start a new class that you can join later.

I also think it'll be good if you can find a place that offers nutrition classes, since you said they don't have them at your club. You said my letters are in-depth and that they are more than enough, but I still think you will benefit from a weekly or monthly programme with a health coach. Your learning style is predominantly kinaesthetic; therefore, finding a place where you can meet with others and engage in practical workshops will encourage you to continue with your new healthy lifestyle. It is so easy to 'fall by the wayside', especially if you don't get instant relief from some of those horrible symptoms. You could be discouraged and give up too soon. However, if you find other people who are on the same journey, you can encourage one another.

In this letter, I want to address some of the issues you raised when we spoke on the phone. I'm sorry to hear about your fatigue and intolerance of noise. Those constant headaches and joint pain are horrible, I know, and that's why I've decided to focus on oxidative stress in this letter.

When I embarked on my journey to find healing, I didn't know it would be a long, arduous one, but the results have been worth it. I took each step in faith and eagerly learnt each lesson. I no longer had to stay indoors because of panic attacks. Other symptoms, like palpitations, head pressure, vertigo, lethargy and insomnia, also became a thing of the past, and my mind became more alert.

Unfortunately, despite my breakthrough in eliminating many symptoms, a persistent problem – aches and pain in my fingers and toes – defied my efforts to get better. Although I no longer had aches in other parts of my body, my fingers and toes continued to feel heavy and painful when I woke up in the morning.

Please understand that I was very grateful that I was healed and had my life back; nevertheless, I wasn't prepared to rest on my oars. I felt ready to enter another phase of my long journey, and I knew I was going to learn more interesting facts about my body.

Lesson 5: Oxidative stress

The next lesson I learnt was about oxidative stress and its effects on the body. What causes it and why is it so damaging to our system? The body depends on oxygen for survival. However, the cells in the body also burn oxygen, which produces free radicals. There are other environmental causes of free radicals, but in this letter, I'd like to focus on the ones that are produced when oxygen is burnt.

The body can detoxify the effects of free radicals by producing antioxidants. Unfortunately, many people do not have enough antioxidants in their system to counteract the damaging effects, and this causes oxidative stress. Scientists have associated the effects of oxidative stress with various motor neuron diseases, premature ageing, cancer, heart disease, Alzheimer's, cancer and chronic joint pain.

My issue at that point was chronic joint pain, and this lesson opened my eyes to the importance of antioxidants and how they can help to neutralise the effects of oxidative stress. The following are some of the things I did; hopefully, you will find them useful.

Eat foods and herbs that are rich in antioxidants

Our planet is blessed with foods that have the power to neutralise free radicals, and so help the body to fight oxidative stress. Milk thistle, turmeric, berries of all types, dark chocolate, black beans and fruits high in vitamin C are excellent sources of antioxidants.

Drink more water

In his book *Your Body's Many Cries for Water: You're Not Sick, You're Thirsty*, physician Fereydoon Batmanghelidj describes water as life-sustaining and life-giving. He attributes most debilitating and so-called incurable diseases to dehydration. The human body is over 75 percent water and only 25 percent solid matter, and the brain, which is extremely sensitive to dehydration, is about 85 percent water. So we need to keep our bodies hydrated continually, otherwise our organs will eventually fail to function properly. When the body is dehydrated, several things occur: constipation, insomnia, lethargy and a host of other illnesses.

For many years, I barely drank up to a litre of water a day. I preferred fizzy drinks full of sugar and other harmful chemicals. An amazing thing happened when I began to drink more water: I felt less bloated and was able to move my bowels daily.

Now, every morning I drink a glass of warm water into which I add the juice of half a lemon – preferably fresh, organic lemon. Sometimes I add crushed ginger or a teaspoon of raw manuka honey. In addition to the health benefits that I get from the lemon, I also get methylglyoxal (MG), the antibacterial component in manuka, which is a good source of antioxidants. Throughout the day, I continue to hydrate my body by drinking pure water. Since doing this, I've had less pain in my joints.

Take apple cider vinegar

There was once a nurse called Margaret Hills who had severe arthritis. She was housebound for several months while receiving conventional treatment until she found a cure. When she became well, she started a clinic for arthritics. She is dead now, but her daughter, Christine Horner, still runs the clinic. One simple remedy that Hills recommends involves apple cider vinegar (ACV), honey, blackstrap molasses and an Epsom salt bath.

Before I found Hills' book, *Treating Arthritis*, I had been using ACV to combat hot flushes, but I decided to strictly follow her regime after reading the testimonies of various people on her website. Twice a day, I drank warm water mixed with a teaspoon of honey and a tablespoon of ACV. I took a teaspoon of blackstrap molasses once or twice a day in my herbal teas. I also had an Epsom salt bath three times a week.

The best type of ACV is Bragg's raw organic apple cider vinegar with the 'mother' in it. The 'mother' are strands of good bacteria, and enzymes. You can actually see the murky strands floating in the bottle. This product helps to regulate the metabolism of your body because it contains many essential minerals. In her book, Hills describes how years of eating a poor diet full of acidic foods leads to hard acid being deposited in people's joints. According to her, ACV has the power to dissolve these acid deposits and they are released from their 'hiding places'.

Natural honey is packed with nutrients like amino acids, magnesium, selenium and a range of B-complex vitamins, and blackstrap molasses is rich in iron, copper and magnesium. Some of these essential minerals are lacking in people who suffer from joint pain. Another important mineral is potassium, which is brilliant for people suffering from panic attacks or anxiety. I found that I was able to sleep better and suffer fewer panic attacks after I started adding these natural foods to my diet, in addition to other healthy, whole foods. There isn't a 'one natural food fits all' solution; a combination of rest, positive thinking, water and essential nutrients works best for most people.

When used in a hot bath, Epsom salts help to remove the acid accumulated in the body by drawing out toxins. I found a good organic brand online, and I add about two scoops to a hot bath and soak in it for about twenty minutes. Then I towel-dry my body and get under my duvet immediately, to encourage acid elimination through sweating. Initially, I found the sweating slightly uncomfortable, but I knew what I wanted to achieve, so it was a minimal price to pay.

I was amazed at how great I felt after just a few days on this regime. The pain in my toes and occasional hot flushes were gone. Although my fingers are still stiff early in the morning, I am determined that one day ALL pain will be a thing of the past.

When the body is full of toxins, everything is out of balance. The symptoms of an imbalanced immune system are devastating, but the way out is not more medication.

Meditate and visualise your breakthrough

In order to heal, I began a new routine every morning: as soon as I woke up, I closed my eyes and visualised how well and wonderful my body felt. In spite of the pains I was having, I kept a picture of wholeness in my mind and I saw myself sharing the story of how I got rid of the pain. I kept that image in my mind until I began to feel excited, then I said my prayers and got out of bed.

That routine was the most effective of all the things I ever did to get better. I say this because every picture that I created in my mind about my wellness became a reality. Every single one of them! It was tempting to keep thinking of the pain; in fact, that was what I'd done for many months. You see, the temptation to obsess about a negative situation and how it may become worse is real. Unfortunately, what we observe and give our attention and energy to manifests. It is easier to wallow in self-pity and talk about our pain than it is to create an unknown future of wholeness.

When I'd had enough of misery, I began to see myself as healthy and happy – drumming, dancing, telling stories and sharing with people how I'd become well. I guess the power to create the future that we want is already within us. Although repeating a diagnosis is normal for most people, I have learnt it will only reinforce the negative condition and draw a pity-party. Well, I did not need such a party; all I wanted was to be healthy and get on with my life. So, visualising and creating my healing worked for me.

My dear, I hope you find the information in this letter helpful. Make sure you eat foods and herbs that are rich in antioxidants, drink more filtered water and check the supermarkets in Lagos for apple cider vinegar – ideally the Bragg brand. If you can't find any, let me know; I'll send you a bottle to start with and we can arrange how you'll get a steady supply. Also, spend time each day meditating and visualising your healing; I find it beneficial.

I look forward to writing to you again. Take care and stay healthy.

Much love,

Wura xx

December 2013

Dear Toriola,

Merry Christmas to you! Thanks very much for your hospitality during my husband's visit to Nigeria. I think the visit was less stressful for him because he had a car and chauffer throughout; he said he used your car for the entire ten days. I really appreciate your help, my friend. My husband also sends his greetings.

I hope you've started using the coconut oil and apple cider vinegar that I sent to you. The key is continuity; you need to use them daily to get the desired results. I'm sure you'll soon be ordering more.

I also sent you a pack of pH strips because I wasn't sure if you'll find them locally. I have just read the letter you sent via my husband, and I will endeavour to answer the questions you asked about why you need the pH strips and how to use them.

Lesson 6: pH Balance

The body is an amazing piece of machinery. Rather than shutting down when it is deficient in an area, it will find ways of compensating for the deficiency by borrowing nutrients or minerals, like calcium, potassium and sodium, from other parts of the body. For example, high acidity, or acidosis, causes the body to take minerals from bones, teeth and organs to prevent the blood from becoming acidic. When the body continues to borrow minerals, conditions like osteoporosis, which is common in women going through menopause, may occur.

Many diseases need an acidic environment to thrive, and the body cannot fight illnesses when its pH is not balanced. Acidosis is also known to be responsible for premature aging, and poor eyesight and memory. Conversely, alkalosis, the opposite of acidosis, could cause cramps, respiratory problems or irritability, due to excess bicarbonate in the blood.

What is pH?

The term 'pH' means the power of hydrogen and it is the measurement of the concentration of hydrogen ions in the body. The pH scale goes from 1 to 14, with 1 being the most acidic. A pH of 7 is neutral, like in pure water, but many people find it difficult to maintain a neutral pH level.

There is no single pH reading for the entire body because various parts have different functions. The digestive tract, for example, has a pH ranging from 1.5 to 7. The skin's pH can be 5.5, which is low on the chart, but the skin needs this slight acidity to fight environmental toxins. The blood is about 7.35 to 7.45, while the stomach's pH varies from 1 to 5, depending on when and what you've eaten. Overall, the body should not be too acidic or alkaline; an ideal balance is between 6.5 and 7.5.

How to measure your body's pH

To find out the body's pH, most people do a urine or saliva test. I found the urine test more accurate. You need the pH strips that I sent you to do this test. Do a saliva or urine test three or four times a day, for seven days. (You will find the instructions in the leaflet inside the packet). Add up the numbers, find the average and record the results.

When I first used these strips, I was not surprised to find out that my pH was low. My body was slightly acidic, which could be the reason for the joint pain I was experiencing. Acidity has been linked to many illnesses and diseases, like cancer, kidney stones, diabetes and osteoporosis, so I knew I had to do something fast.

Getting the balance right

A balanced diet that consists of a variety of acid and alkaline forming foods is crucial to having a balanced pH. However, it is not enough to simply put foods into categories of acidic or alkaline. For example, lemon is naturally acidic, but when it gets into your stomach it becomes alkaline; hence, it's great to take lemon with warm water in the morning. You can also add a hint of lemon to water throughout the day. Another example is milk. In its natural form it is not acidic, but when milk gets into the body it becomes acidic. So it's important to find out what foods turn into when they are broken down and reach the stomach.

To get a balanced diet, I included a helping of green leafy vegetables and fruits of various colours in my diet through juicing and smoothie-making. I later learnt how to make nice raw dishes.

God did not create a woman's body to break down because of age or season of life. Perimenopause should not be synonymous with aches and pains or negative conditions; I am convinced that the horrors of perimenopause were never in the original plan for us. There is a pathway that leads to many of the symptoms and there is a pathway out of them.

I don't know what story the world will tell women about perimenopause in the future. They may create more dangerous drugs for those who are going through the season. But I want you to know that the pathway to health is already laid out for you; all you need to do is follow it.

Toriola, I hope my explanation of pH balance is clear. Please don't hesitate to ask questions if you need more information, and do let me know how you get on with the pH testing.

I look forward to hearing from you soon.

Take care and be blessed.

Much love,

Wura xx

January 2014

My dear Toriola,

Happy New Year! Thanks for your phone call yesterday; it was lovely to hear from you. Hope you're settling back into work after that ordeal. Goodness, what a way to start a new year! I have been thinking about our conversation and I feel deeply sad that you've had to go through all that alone. I didn't realise how bad the situation was; I know Fikayo has never been there for you, but this?

Anyway, my main concern is not Fikayo. He has chosen his own pathway and decided to have another family; there isn't much you can do about it. YOU are my main concern. I'm worried about your state of mind and the decisions you're making. I don't think going to confront Fikayo and his new family is the way forward. What do you hope to achieve by that?

We all know you love Fikayo, but I think it's time you started to take care of yourself and focus on Remilekun and Maria. They are your jewels of inestimable value and you know they love you to bits. Let's be thankful for them and let Fikayo live his life the way he pleases. Perhaps one day his eyes will open and he will see the damage he has done to his own family. In the meantime, you need to focus on positive thoughts instead of your marital problems. Also, please stop blaming yourself! The only thing I'm hearing from you is guilt. Why are you blaming yourself because your husband abandons you and your children, starts another family, breezes in and out of your life and dumps you again?

I know it's not easy to take your mind off a negative situation, but if only for the sake of your sanity and your children, you need to try to do so. It is great to know that you're now on WhatsApp; let's speak regularly, even if it's once a week. I'm not happy that you're carrying this burden alone. How's Aunty Kanyinsola? Is she still in Lagos? I haven't heard you talk about her in ages. I know you had a row a few years ago; do you still communicate with her? Perhaps being an older sibling, she may be a shoulder to cry on if you need someone with whom to sit down and have a chat.

You may be wondering why I'm going on about getting rid of negative thoughts. I don't think we humans really understand the effects of negative emotions on the body, so when we are plagued with feelings of worry, guilt, insecurity, bitterness, hatred, envy or anger, we either ignore them, thinking they will just go away, or we think the emotions are only located in the mind, so there's nothing to worry about. Unfortunately, a toxic emotion is like a trap set in the yard of the mind; it may seem less dangerous because it isn't a visible illness or condition, but it is deadly.

I'd like to pause here to tell you a story that a friend shared with me a few years ago:

Story: The rat trap

Once upon a time, there was a rat who lived with his family in a crevice of a wall in a farmhouse. One day he heard a commotion and he quickly went to see what was happening.

He saw the farmer and his wife arguing.

'That is very wicked', the farmer said.

'I really don't care', his wife retorted. 'I want that stinking rat and his family to disappear'! Then she proceeded to set a rat trap.

'Ouch, a rat trap'! the rat cried, and he quickly went out to the fields to find the chicken. 'There's a rat trap in the yard'! he yelled.

The chicken eyed him incredulously. 'So what if there's a rat trap in the yard? It's called a *rat* trap, not a chicken trap', he scoffed.

The rat quietly retreated and went to look for the pig. 'There's a rat trap in the yard'! he shouted.

The pig snorted, 'Hmm, well, I'm sorry to hear that. You and your family are in my prayers'. The pig walked away from the rat.

The rat was exasperated. 'Oh dear, what else can I do? I know, I'll go find the cow'. He ran into a field and soon spotted the cow eating grass. 'Cow'! he called. 'There's a rat trap in the farmyard'.

The cow lifted his head. 'Oh really, a rat trap? I'm shivering all over, my friend. Rat trap, rat trap, help me, everyone'! He mooed dramatically, and the other farm animals fell about laughing. The rat went back to his home, dejected.

Later that night, a loud clang echoed throughout the farmyard. The farmer's wife was delighted; she thought the rat had been caught, so she hurried towards the crevice. Unfortunately, the trap had caught a venomous snake and it bit her. She was rushed to the hospital, but the doctors could not help her, so she came back home with a terrible fever.

When the neighbours came to see her, the farmer took his

machete and went into the yard to look for some ingredients to make soup. The main ingredient was chicken. Everyone ate and the neighbours went back to their houses.

The woman did not get better, so her family travelled to see her. Again, the farmer went into the yard, and this time he slaughtered the pig and served the entire family hot pork chops.

A few days later, the farmer's wife died, and many people came to commiserate with the farmer. On the day of the funeral, the farmer asked his friends to butcher the cow and a feast was prepared for the visitors.

At dusk, the rat came out of his tiny home and looked around the empty farmyard. 'What a strange world', he mused. 'Indeed, when there is a rat trap in the yard, everyone on the farm is at risk'! He shook his head and went back into his home.

My dear Toriola, in this story the farm animals did not understand that everything is connected. Similarly, when there's a toxic emotion floating around in your mind, your entire body is at risk. Neuroscientist Dr Caroline Leaf, in her seminars, talks about eliminating toxic emotions. She said they could clog up the neural pathways in the brain and that this eventually causes tangled tau proteins. These tangled proteins could lead to physical and mental trauma, including motor neurone diseases and Alzheimer's. It is therefore important to dig out mind toxins as soon as possible.

Lesson 7: Dig out negative emotions

Toxic emotions are dangerous to the body and must always be treated as alien. Eating healthily and exercising are good habits, but there's no amount of broccoli or lemon that can remove toxic emotions. Good thoughts and a healthy mind are the body's primary food; every other thing is secondary.

Scientists have always divided the human body into 'neck up' and 'neck down'. The specialists for the former are called mental health practitioners, while practitioners that deal with the latter are physicians. However, the entire body network is linked. Here's a personal story to explain this further:

One day, I noticed I was having terrible pains in my right shoulder and I thought I had strained it during a routine exercise. However, when the pain did not subside and I began to have excruciating pain in my right armpit as well, I went to the hospital. The doctors did an X-ray and various tests and they told me they couldn't find anything wrong. I was distraught; nevertheless, I knew there was another lesson for me to learn.

A few days after my hospital visit, I lay down to pray and meditate. I asked my body why it was harbouring pain. What happened next was baffling; it was as if I was getting an answer right there and then. The answer sounded like, *Ask the pain why it is present in your body.* Thank God I was alone, so I spoke out loud: 'Pain, why are you tormenting me'? I didn't hear any voice, but an answer was firmly imprinted in my mind: *It is because of your fear of poverty.*

I sat up in bed! Until then, I had not realised that in my subconscious there was a fear that I may not be able to earn enough through my work and business. At that time, I had stopped lecturing at the university and was freelancing. However, work wasn't coming in as it used to, and I was afraid that my meagre income might not be enough to meet my financial responsibilities.

That day, I started a 21-day 'brain detox' and began to flush out all thoughts of failure. The pain in my armpit stopped, but I was still having some discomfort in my right shoulder, so I went on a seven-day prayer and meditation programme. Each night over the seven days I anointed my shoulder with oil and spoke directly to it. I said: 'Shoulder, I relieve you of pain, because my healing is already paid for. Jesus carried a cross on His shoulder; that must have been very painful. I don't need to carry any pain on my shoulder; therefore, I am healed'.

One evening after the seven days of prayer, I went to a meeting, and by the time I came back the pain had spread to my elbow and I was in agony. A new community project was starting the following day, and I went to bed wondering how I would be able to carry all my musical instruments to the venue.

That night I had a dream. I saw a man coming towards me with two helpers. He laid his left hand on my shoulder and with the other hand he pulled out a lump from my armpit. When I woke up I was totally pain-free. I lifted my right hand above my head, put it across my chest to touch my left shoulder and felt no pain. I hadn't been able to do that for about eight months! Before I went out that day, I pulled out my diary and wrote about the miraculous experience.

Letting go of negative emotions and fear could be the first step towards healing. Prayer releases the power of God, which sets you free from any form of trauma. I am a living witness! I have been telling this story ever since. Some people believe me, but some are cynical. However, I don't tell my story because I want to prove anything; I share it as an offering of thanksgiving for my healing. I am telling you this story to encourage you not to give up, but to keep praying and hoping for your miracle.

My dear friend, you have been through a lot in the past two years, but I implore you to dig out the root of your negative emotions and ask for wisdom and strength to wade these waters. I hope this letter has encouraged you to keep moving on. I look forward to writing to you shortly. In the meantime, take care of yourself and be happy.

Much love,

Wura xx

February 2014

Dear Toriola,

I got your letter today, and am I excited or what? I am thrilled that you have decided to visit us here in England during your annual leave. Wow, wow, wow! I don't even know what to say right now. I know it's still a few months before your visit, but I can't wait to have you in my house! There are millions of things to catch up on, my friend.

I'm happy to hear that you eventually went to see your GP after that nasty episode. Well, I'm not surprised that she's placed you on tranexamic acid; she wouldn't want you to bleed to death. Heavy periods are one of the horrors that some women experience during perimenopause.

In answer to your question, yes, apart from tranexamic acid there are a few other medical treatments available to women who are going through perimenopause if menstruation is disruptive because it is too heavy or it lasts too long. One is endometrial ablation, a minor operation in which the lining of the uterus is burned. There's also the option of using an IUCD called Mirena, which releases progestin and helps to reduce blood flow. Some researchers say Mirena reduces menstrual flow by about 90 percent. Ask your doctor about these other treatments and let me know what she suggests to you. Also, do your research about each and decide what you want.

You asked if I have used any of them. Yes, I have. As I mentioned in one of my earlier letters, I took tranexamic acid for many years, but I reached a point where it was no longer effective in the first three days of my period.

One day I went to visit a friend. She was a great hostess and created a calming ambiance in her guest room for me. Everything was white. I was so tired, I fell asleep as soon as my head hit the pillow and I slept through the night, on my back. When I woke up, I found that the bedsheet and mattress were drenched in red – totally soaked through. That was after I had taken tranexamic acid four times the day before and worn a multi-layered sanitary towel. It was as if my erratic, heavy period sat on one side of the bed mocking me and defying my 'acid' tablets and Kilimanjaro pad.

Even though my friend was sympathetic, I was irritated like an open wound! I sat indoors all day, muttering in pidgin mingled with Yoruba: 'Wetin? Wetin happen gangan? To be woman na curse? Ki lo de gangan'? Toriola, I'd better translate this, because I know you can hardly read Yoruba, ha ha ha! My rant went thus: 'What is it? What exactly is happening? Is it a curse to be a woman? What exactly is it'?

When I left my friend's house, I drove to my GP's surgery, and after he had listened to my bitter complaint, he asked the nurse to fit me with a Mirena coil. From the word go, my body rejected it, but the nurse managed to put it in. That was the biggest mistake of my adult life! My period went barking mad, and the coil eventually slipped out of me like a frightened little mouse tiptoeing away from a sleeping cat.

I went back to my GP, and he referred me to a specialist, who suggested I consider endometrial ablation. I called all my 'gynae' friends and asked for their advice. I didn't get any clarity; some were for and some were against it for various reasons. That was when fear set in. I had chronic anaemia and often felt light-headed.

I began to pray for guidance. I don't want to bleed to death, but I had a strong feeling that I shouldn't go for surgery. I increased my water intake to hydrate my body, and I ate foods that are rich in vitamin C and iron. These helped to keep my body balanced and they made the flow a little less heavy, but I still needed a breakthrough.

One morning on my way to work, I tuned in to a YouTube channel that I'd recently discovered. Bruce Lipton, a cellular biologist, was being interviewed and he said we should be speaking to our cells because they are listening to us. I was so excited I wanted to scream! It was as if Bruce was giving me scientific facts backing up the first lesson I had learnt on my healing journey: 'Your body is a living organism, speak to it'. I listened to him as he described epigenetics in layman's terms.

What I did next was not conventional, but it gave me the breakthrough that I was yearning for. I will share this with you. First, though, let me tell you the story of a woman who lived in the 1st century AD, but whose tale is still told widely in our world today. Her story came to my mind as I prepared for my breakthrough.

Story: The woman who kept bleeding

There was once a woman who had suffered haemorrhages for 12 years. She had gone to many doctors and paid so much money in her search for healing, but no one could help her. This woman lived in the Middle East, in a culture where women were not allowed out in public when they had their period. However, she heard that the healer, Jesus Christ, was passing through her town and she made up her mind to go to him and be healed.

That day, she left her house and joined the crowd in the market place. She said in her heart, *If I could only touch the hem of his garment, I will be healed.* When she got close enough to Jesus, she stretched out her hand and touched his garment. Instantly, she stopped haemorrhaging.

Then Jesus looked around and said, 'Who touched me'? The people around Him were surprised to hear that question. Peter, one of the disciples, felt the question was ridiculous.

'But Master', he said, 'there are so many people around us; dozens have touched you'.

'No, this is different', Jesus answered him. 'I felt power discharging from me'.

The woman knew she couldn't hide any longer and she came to Jesus and told her story.

Jesus said to her, 'Daughter, your faith has healed you; go in peace'.

I read this story in the Book of Luke, a physician and writer, and one of the disciples of Jesus. What intrigues me about this woman's story is her faith. 'If I could only touch the hem of his garment'...

I meditated on the woman's faith and her determination to find healing at all costs, notwithstanding tradition. Her faith made me feel energised and I focused on one thing: that my heavy periods would become normal again. I then began to speak to my body. I focused on what I wanted - normal periods without heavy bleeding.

One morning, while meditating, I felt the need to fast and pray for three days. I didn't know why I felt that nudge to pray, but I was desperate for a breakthrough.

On the first day, as I began to pray, I sensed I needed to be quiet in God's presence. Initially, I ignored that prompting and continued to complain about my numerous issues. The way I'd been taught to pray was to keep asking God to take away whatever problem I had; it felt strange to be quiet when I was meant to pray. For me, prayer is about pouring out your heart, especially when you need a breakthrough on certain issues.

Nevertheless, I was eager to heed the nudging in my spirit, so I knelt beside my bed and closed my eyes. Although I was not speaking, my mind was anything but silent. I wasn't used to this type of 'silent' praying and it didn't feel natural; I needed to talk about my frustrations.

After a few hours, I calmed down and meditated on Isaiah 53:5 'But he was pierced for our transgressions, he was crushed for our iniquities; the punishment that brought us peace was on him, and by his wounds we are healed'. Then I began to say 'Amen' because suddenly it was as if someone was praying over me. So I stopped complaining and silently meditated on scriptures. It wasn't an easy task, because occasionally I slipped into my old habits, but I quickly refocused.

By the second day, I had become quieter and I stayed focused for longer before getting distracted. I continued my meditation and gradually stopped feeling frustrated. Also, the battle I had with doubt and unbelief was not as fierce as before. Each time my mind projected fear and doubt, I quickly fought back with counter-narratives. I read and reread stories like the one I shared earlier from the Book of Luke, and these narratives stirred up faith in me and gave me the strength to continue my fast.

On the third day, whilst praying, I saw a vision of a man building an altar in the middle of an empty room. Then I heard the words, 'The Lord your God in your midst, The Mighty One, will save'. I felt a profound sense of peace, and then I let go of my fears. In her '21-Day Brain Detox Programme', Dr Caroline Leaf talks about first giving thanks and then visualising yourself standing before God and releasing your fears one by one. I put this into practice and named my fears one by one, saying aloud, 'I hand this matter over to you, Lord'. I shifted my focus from my condition and focused on my healing.

Fear is the root of many afflictions. It was initially difficult for me to let go of fear; its root was deep. There must be a reason why the admonition not to fear appears more than 364 times in the Bible. It seems we need to repeat it to ourselves every day.

Fear is a silent killer. It makes you lose every sense of reason, makes you weak and fuels unbelief. It can trap you in a vicious circle: first, you're afraid you will have a condition, then you have the condition, then you are afraid of dying from the condition, and then you start all over again. Fear is demonic!

During that fast, there were many times when I nearly gave up. My mind chatter was explosive: '*How can you expect to be healed from something that is natural? Every woman goes through it; why should your situation be any different*'? However, after three days of prayer and meditation, I felt stabilised. I felt safe. The shift in focus was bearing fruit; I was becoming what I was thinking about: a healthy, fearless being. I was entering the place where I was meant to be; I was coming out of the dungeon of despondency.

For the first time in many months, I could give thanks again. Until then, the fear of not knowing what was happening to me and where it would lead had kept me from singing praises or being thankful; my focus was totally on my symptoms. Now each month, instead of anticipating a heavy period, I visualised that it would be light and painless. I imagined that I would sleep well and wouldn't need to use numerous pills. Soon, what I imagined began to happen! It was a miraculous breakthrough. Some might say that menopause had eventually set in and that is why my periods changed. However, I say that as soon as I began to visualise what I wanted for my body, I had peace. I stopped taking tranexamic acid almost immediately and my periods went back to normal.

When you experience a breakthrough, your faith soars! It is like feedback that encourages you to believe more and continue to have faith. My dear friend, you have nothing to lose by making visualisation part of your daily routine. It is like opening a new neural pathway in the brain and shutting down the old fear-based route.

My dear, I hope this letter has been helpful. Please look out for my next letter.

Much love,

Wura xx

March 2014

Dear Toriola,

How are you? My family and I are well, and spring is here at last! I saw the first daffodil bloom today on my way to the local 'one-stop-shop', and I couldn't help muttering, 'Times and seasons are appointed to all'.

How are your children? My Ade is sorely disappointed that her 'Volunteer in Africa' trip to Sierra Leone was cancelled. I tried to talk to her, but she's behaving unreasonably! I thought a girl of her age would understand the organisers' point of view. Ebola is sweeping through Sierra Leone as we speak; it would be irresponsible for the organisers not to cancel the trip. We had a heated argument this morning and she left the house in tears. Oh, I feel so frustrated! Did we behave like that when we were their age? Can you imagine talking back to your mum? I can't.

Anyway, writing to you today makes me feel better. I got your letter two days ago. It was quite short, unlike your usual long letters. Are you okay, my friend? I hope you're not keeping anything from me. Are the children okay?

You said you've had to take time off work because you couldn't sleep well. Are you still using the sleeping pills prescribed for you, and are they helping?

I battled with insomnia for many years, but I now sleep so

well that I have to set an alarm to wake me up. I did a few things to regulate my sleeping pattern; I'll share them below.

In your letter, you said I should explain a phrase that I used when we talked on the phone some weeks ago. I said, 'It is an abomination for the horse to ride the rider.' I will explain, but first I want to share a story with you.

Story: The butterfly

A young man decided to play a trick on an elderly man who was regarded as the wisest in the region. One morning he went to visit the old man, and on his way he caught a butterfly and cupped it in his palms.

'I'll ask the old man if this butterfly is alive or dead', he soliloquised. 'If he says it is alive, I will crush it and kill it, but if he says it is dead, I will let the butterfly loose. Then he'll not be such a wise man, will he'?

When he got to the elder, he bowed and greeted him: 'Good morning, wise one'.

'Greetings, my son, please sit down. What brings you to my house so early'?

'Sir,' said the young man, 'I have a butterfly in my hands. Is it dead or alive'?

The old man smiled as he gazed at the youth. 'It depends on you, my son. Whether that butterfly is alive or dead is your decision; the power lies in your hands'.

The young man turned around and trudged home with his head bowed.

This story illustrates the point that I want to highlight in this letter, which is a lesson I learnt when I was battling insomnia. At that time, I struggled to fall asleep, and sometimes when I did, I couldn't stay asleep for longer than one or two hours. This impacted both my work and social life. I yawned almost every minute and fell asleep during meetings at work.

One day in class, I asked my students to read out their creative writing pieces, and as they did I fell asleep. That was an unforgivable sin in the classroom and my students showed no mercy! They complained that I was incompetent when they wrote their feedback on the end-of-term evaluation form. Life was becoming hard, and I had no one to turn to. I soon realised that perimenopause is not a topic that most women happily discuss. Anytime I tried to bring up the topic people quickly changed the subject.

Things went from bad to worse and I could hardly concentrate on anything. I started forgetting people's names, even my colleagues'. I had to write everything down on paper. The worst times were during conversations. I knew what I wanted to say, but words eluded me, and I'd just stand there 'uming' and 'erming' like a moron. Sometimes when I called my children to send them on errands, by the time they got to where I was, I would have forgotten what I wanted to say to them. This continued for a few years, and it was mental torture.

One of my lowest points was when one morning, after many sleepless nights, I saw one of my colleagues but didn't recognise her. I called her by another person's name and thought she was that person throughout our conversation. Later, I wondered why she had given me such a strange look, and I realised my mistake. At that point, I thought I was losing the plot. I took time off work, knowing I had to sort myself out.

One night, a few weeks after I'd stopped work, I had a strange dream that left a lasting impression on me.

A horse and its rider – a dream

In my dream, I saw a horse riding a man. The man was carrying the horse on his head! The horse held a whip and it struck the man very hard and yelled, 'Hey ho'!

When I woke up, I wondered what the strange dream meant. Later, as I was meditating, it was as if I was interpreting my own dream.

I am a spirit being who's been given a wonderful body so that I can live on planet earth. However, just as a horse should not mount and ride a human being, my body should not be the boss, dictating to me. I should nurture and take care of it, but it should not control me. Whenever it begins to go out of sync, I should call it back to order, gently but firmly, with good nutrients, prayer and positive words. Through your words, life or death can be released; your words carry authority and power over your body.

This lesson was not an easy one to learn, but eventually, after trial and error, stumbling, falling and getting up again, I mastered it. The story of the man and the butterfly helped me to understand the imagery of the horse and its rider better. Sickness may knock on the door of my body, but there are two ways to respond: I can open the door and make it comfortable by complaining about it, or I can shut the door in its face and tell it where to go – it is up to me. Saint Mark described faith thus: 'Truly I tell you, if anyone says to this mountain, "Go throw yourself into the sea", and does not doubt in their heart but believes that what they say will happen, it will be done for them' (Mark 11:23).

According to a Yoruba proverb, 'You may not be able to stop a bird from defecating on your head, but you can stop it from building a nest in your hair'. In the Genesis narrative, before God called the earth into order, it was dark and formless. Nevertheless, God did not call His team to discuss the darkness; rather, He spoke order into the universe: 'let there be light'. He decided what He wanted to see and declared it.

Perhaps you're thinking, but that's God, the creator of heaven and earth. I agree with you; however, God made us in His likeness and gave us the authority to bring order to the chaos in our lives. Paul said in his letter to the Ephesians (5:1): 'Be imitators of God'. You can imitate God by speaking 'life' into any negative situation.

Your thoughts and words are powerful. There is no such thing as an idle thought or word; you become what you think or talk about. You may not be able to stop an illness attacking you, but you can stop it pitching a permanent tent inside your body, which is the temple of God.

Overcoming insomnia

How did I finally overcome insomnia? The first thing I did was to examine my sleep pattern to know what type of problems I was experiencing. I battled with two issues. Firstly, I found it difficult to fall asleep easily, and even when I did, I woke up in the middle of the night and couldn't get back to sleep for a few hours. The second problem was that I was not having a good, restful sleep even when I slept. I got up frequently with the urge to visit the bathroom, and after that I tossed and turned all night. In the morning, I felt tired and sleepy and was useless to everyone, even myself!

There are various other types of sleep problems, but these were the ones that were bothering me. After I identified mine, I started researching the causes of insomnia. Having healed a few other ailments, I knew I couldn't just depend on doctors to 'drug me up' with sleeping pills; all I wanted was to get to the root of the issues.

I started by addressing my routine. I stopped using my laptop and mobile phone after eight p.m. and read a good book instead of staring at a screen. I tried to go to sleep and wake up at about the same time every day. Before then, I had slept anytime I wanted, and I went to bed as late as one or two in the morning. I changed that and went to bed by ten p.m. at the latest. Some days I used magnesium oil – four sprays on each thigh just before going to bed. Come the morning, no matter how tired I was, I got up, did some light exercise and followed my lemon water and juicing regime. I also noticed that when I juiced celery religiously, like nearly every day, I slept much better.

During my research, I found out that insomnia isn't just a thyroid problem; it can be caused by toxic heavy metals in the brain, a sluggish liver, viruses, sleep apnoea or adrenal issues. Most of the toxins that affect the body can also affect our sleep. I intensified my juicing, especially pure celery juice. I took at least 16 ounces each morning and followed it up with a 'heavy metal detox smoothie'. That consists of two cups of organic frozen wild blueberries, a handful of fresh coriander leaves, one teaspoon each of spirulina and barley grass juice powder, a handful of dulse and two ripe bananas. I got the recipe from the website of Anthony William, a holistic health coach.

The next thing I did was to stop talking about insomnia as if I was still having the issue. I began to talk about what I wanted, which meant I created a story in my mind about a time when I would be able to sleep soundly and refreshingly. Every night before I slept, I pulled out my book of affirmations and chanted a few phrases. In the past when I couldn't sleep, I would lie on the bed thinking of numerous problems. I soon changed this habit and either read a book or read aloud my affirmations. Here are some of them:

- When I lie down, I will not be afraid; when I lie down, my sleep will be sweet.
- He (God) grants sleep to those He loves.
- In peace I will lie down and sleep, for you alone, Lord, make me dwell in safety.

Gradually, my sleeping pattern improved, and I began to sleep for longer until the insomnia was history. You can see from the story I've shared in this letter that it was a combination of several interventions that made the difference. Whatever the 'magic' answer out of them was, it's just great to be able to sleep soundly at night! It's as if everything depends on quality sleep. A good night's sleep is life-enhancing.

My dear friend, I look forward to writing to you soon. Be happy.

Much love,

Wura xx

April 2014

Dear Toriola,

I'm sorry to have missed your call last week. I called back a few times, but I couldn't reach you, so I sent you a text. I hope you received my message. I got your letter yesterday, and I'm happy to know that the tinnitus has subsided and you are regaining your strength.

How are your lovely children? In your letter, you said they now visit their dad regularly. Well done, my friend, thumbs up to you. I imagine it wasn't easy for you to make that decision, but I am happy you found enough courage to do what needs to be done. As you said in your letter, the children love their father and he is a good dad, even though he's a lousy husband. I'm excited to hear that Maria is happier and that both of you are now communicating better.

It's great to hear that our correspondence is uplifting for you. I have fantastic news to share with you. A client with whom I've been working for a few months called me this morning. She has been trying to get pregnant for four years and she called to say that she's now six weeks pregnant! I can't share the details of her coaching with you, but the reason I'm mentioning it in this letter is because my client and I worked on a principle that I feel may be of benefit to you. I'll call it Lesson 8…

Lesson 8: Praise therapy

Thanksgiving is not something we should do only when we are happy and everything is going well. I learnt how to sing songs of praise when I was ill and had no hope. I gave thanks for everything and still found more reasons to be thankful. Initially, it felt strange to be positive when my health wasn't sound. However, the truth was that despite my predicament I was still able to feed myself, take care of my family and even do some part-time work, so I chose to focus on that and give thanks for my family, my home and the food on my table.

Every morning, after I'd had my juice, I started a praise marathon, and it made me feel light-hearted. The experience was surreal. It was as if I'd been lost in a strange wilderness and had found a guide who was going to lead me out, and the guide was telling me that everything would be all right.

After a few days of constant praise and worship anywhere and everywhere, it became a habit. I found that 'praise therapy' helped me to win the battle over sadness and mood swings. When I was praising and thinking about good and pleasant things, I was never sad. One day I gave thanks for a £3.75 coupon that I got after paying for my groceries. That meagre amount won't change my life, but I had mastered the art of thanksgiving, and that will eventually save my life.

After many days of the praise marathon, my body began to respond to my words; I was getting stronger and happier. Each time the dark cloud of sadness loomed, I stood in front of a mirror and said to myself, 'I have boundless joy; I am so happy; my joy is contagious'. Within a few minutes I would feel the pressure lifting. Getting such results made it easier to continue. I practised this every single day, no matter how I felt.

Soon, I regained a zest for life. I was mastering the art of thanksgiving and it was a great feeling. I had not experienced such a real and deep sense of God's presence for many years. His presence was tangible to me, more than any other thing. I'd be lying if I told you that life was rosy from that time on; some days were better than others but I did not give up. Every day I had the opportunity to go on an adventure just practising the new lesson I'd learnt.

Gradually, I regained my strength. I ate well, hydrated with water, took long walks and exercised every day. I made a conscious effort to screen the thoughts that I allowed my mind to focus on, and I am truly blessed because of that decision.

My dear friend, try 'praise therapy' and let me know about your experience. I look forward to your letter.

Much love,

Wura xx

May 2014

Dear Toriola,

I received your letter a week ago and I planned to write back to you immediately, but I was preparing for a conference. I read your letter with great joy and danced around my kitchen. I didn't even realise my husband was standing behind me, laughing. Such great news! I am delighted by what you called your 'first little miracle of sleep'. My dear, no miracle is 'little'.

How amazing that you're gradually sleeping better at night. If after months of insomnia you can get a good night's sleep, it is worth celebrating. Sleep is very important; when you win the battle with insomnia, many other problems will be resolved.

I can't believe we're counting the weeks until you arrive in Blighty – hooray! This is going to be the last letter you'll receive from me before you visit us in England, and it is with great pleasure that I conclude our series of letters. When you said that you have a file where you keep all my letters and that you have read them multiple times, I felt humbled. I am so happy that I could be of help to you during these challenging times, and I thank you for the regular feedback you've sent to me each month.

The lessons I have shared with you gave me a new lease of

life. As I mentioned earlier in one of my letters, I am not attributing the word disease to perimenopause; however, for some women, their perimenopause experience is worse than a disease because perimenopause has the potential to render a woman's body weak and susceptible to other illnesses. A person may go to the hospital with a heart condition, and the doctors will focus on the issue. However, for some women who are going through perimenopause, their entire system is affected. The good news is that women do not have to continue to endure these issues. There is a pathway to deliverance.

I learnt that my body is a living organism with ears and that I must speak life to it. I now understand the importance of strengthening my immune system, and I know about the negative effects of toxins in the body and how to detoxify to bring my body back to homeostasis. It was also exciting to gain knowledge about stress and pH balance. I don't think there are enough words to describe how much I'm enjoying life presently. The lessons on the importance of moving the body more, digging out the root of negative emotions, changing my narrative and controlling my thoughts were invaluable, to say the least. Lastly, I learnt how to do a mind detox through prayer and praise. These lessons are as effective today as when I first learnt them. I now understand that I have the power to choose which narratives I allow into my conscious mind.

The mini narratives

Over 33,000 mini narratives clamour for your attention each day. Although they come in the form of thoughts and occupy your subconscious, each of them, like a tiny sperm trying to win the egg fertilisation race, is pressing towards your conscious mind, hoping to be the lucky one you choose to process. A few of them, perhaps less than 2 percent, will eventually find their way into your conscious mind because you choose to focus on them. Now here's the interesting bit: you have the power to give life to these mini stories and make them into a full narrative, and whatever power you give to them, they will wield it over you.

The unnatural perimenopause is contrary to the plan of the creator; therefore, I needed to align myself with the real story. I crafted a new story for myself, and here it is: *I am a healthy woman whose body was under attack. However, I now know the pathway to health, and I am walking on it and getting stronger and happier every day.*

This new story became my 'truth', and I focused on it instead of the lies plaguing my mind. Those oppressive lies came to me as mini narratives every day. The list was endless: *your brain fog will lead to early-onset dementia*; *your panic attacks will never stop*; *you will bleed to death, because as you can see, the tablets are not even working*; *this perimenopause thing has no cure*; *how will you get out of this situation since the doctors can't find anything wrong with you?*; *it is better not to be ill because healing rarely happens these days…*

As soon as I grasped the truth, I began to take captive every thought, just like Paul declared in his second letter to the people of Corinth: 'The weapons of our warfare are not carnal, but mighty through God to pull down strongholds. Casting down imaginations and every high thing that exalts itself against the knowledge of God and bringing into captivity every thought to the obedience of Christ' (2 Corinthians 10:4–6).

When you are dealing with mind chatter, speaking positive

words is not enough to get rid of negative thoughts. They are strongholds and their mission is to cripple you because once you believe the lies, no medicine can cure you. To be totally set free, you need to deal with those mini stories. You need to start telling your body the true story and repeating it until new neural pathways of this truth are formed in your brain. Your body will respond to you because you are the rider of the horse – your body. The horse is not meant to ride the rider.

The words that we speak over our negative mind chatter matter a lot because they are potent. Many times it's as if we need divine help to overcome the negativity that cripples the mind. If we want divine help, we must understand that our fears do not move God; only His words move Him to action and He watches over them to make sure they are fulfilled.

Telling the true story

The most effective way to change your narrative is to find out the true story about your life and then tell it. The story about what you are created to do and how you'll do it is written in a book. The psalmist described it succinctly in the following words: 'All the days ordained for me were written in your book before one of them came to be. How precious to me are your thoughts, God! How vast the sum of them' (Psalm 139: 16–17).

When you know what is written about your destiny, you can focus on your mission here on earth. You are not a cosmic accident; your story started as a thought in the creator's mind and He wrote it down before you'd lived a single day of your life. After your time here on earth, you'll be asked about your journey based on what was written in your book. Here's how John described it in Revelation (20:12): 'And I saw the dead, great and small, standing before the throne, and books were opened. Also, another book was opened, which is the book of life. And the dead were judged by what was written in the books, by what they had done'.

Accessing your book – the gift of vision

Whilst your physical eyes deal with sight – helping you to see the beauty all around; helping you to avoid falling into a ditch – your spiritual eyes deal with *vision*. They see your purpose and how to fulfil it. They see dreams, prophetic signs, and visions of the future and how to get through a difficult situation. Unfortunately, this powerful gift of vision is ignored by many people.

It is with the spiritual eyes that you see and read from the book that the psalmist describes in Psalm 139. Reading about one's life assignment is a profound experience.

There are times when you receive a vision or a dream that stirs you up. Some people become very passionate about a cause and they won't rest until they do something about it. Others may feel led to carry out a project. That inclination is like a whisper in their ears. Here's how the prophet Isaiah describes it: 'And your ears shall hear a word behind you, saying, "This is the way, walk in it"' (30:21).

I was in my early twenties when I had a vivid vision about my purpose, or what some may call my mission. From that time onward I prayed for the wisdom and understanding to carry it out. Unfortunately, when I became ill my focus shifted from my assignment to my predicament, especially when I became weak, physically and emotionally.

Going through this journey, I have learnt to refocus and to know that while I'm still working on my assignment, no devil from hell can snuff out my light. I revisited the vision I had in my twenties as if reading the book of my life again, and I started planning new strategies for how to carry it out effectively and successfully.

Immediately after I refocused, my body responded positively. The sense of malaise that had plagued me for many months gave way to a feeling of joy and wellness. Each day I woke up looking forward to a wonderful, fun-filled day, instead of the doom and gloom that I had experienced. Indeed, the body is a living organism with ears, and it responds to whatever you say to it – good or bad.

It's time to tell your story

When you know the story that the creator has written about you, it is easy to tell it through your work, profession or ministry. Every day when you wake up, reinforce this story to counter the lies that plague your mind. You may not be able to stop the mini narratives that come to your subconscious mind, but you can decide which one you give life to, or which one occupies a space in your conscious mind. Reinforce your story through repetition; it is the best way to reprogram your subconscious mind and align it to God's plan for your life.

Your mind is a battlefield between doubt and faith. However, YOU determine who wins. The lessons that I have been sharing with you for the past eighteen months created a new pathway to health and vitality for me, and I will continue to cherish them. The journey was long and arduous. It was four years of navigating dark alleys, treacherous mountains, low valleys and muddy waters. Nevertheless, I am excited to tell you that I overcame every debilitating symptom. My greatest joy is that I can share the story of my healing journey with you.

My experience, though tough and painful, opened my eyes to the difference between natural and unnatural perimenopause. I believe that God's will for every woman is for her to prosper, whatever her age. The great news is that a woman has the power to choose the pathway to health so that when she enters the season of perimenopause, her body will have the strength to go through it peacefully.

I would like to share a final story with you.

Story: Jacob and the speckled animals

Once upon a time, there was a man called Jacob. He cheated his older brother, Esau, of his birthright by tricking their father into blessing him instead of his brother. Esau became very angry and vowed to kill Jacob once their aged father died. Their mother told Jacob to flee to his uncle, Laban, and live with him until Esau's anger subsided.

Jacob fled to his uncle's house, where he prospered and became wealthy. Laban was jealous of the young man's business acumen and cheated him a few times, but Jacob continued to serve his uncle, who later became his father-in-law. After many years, Jacob decided it was time for them to part ways, and the two men agreed that Jacob should take every speckled or spotted sheep and lamb as his wages.

Jacob then did something outstanding to increase his flocks. He took freshly cut poplar, almond and plane branches and created white stripes on them by peeling the bark and exposing the inner white wood of the branches. Then he placed them in the watering troughs so that the sheep would stare at the branches when they came to drink and mate. The sheep then bore speckled or spotted animals, and so Jacob's flocks increased.

Jacob became prosperous and owned large flocks. He later bade his father-in-law farewell and went back to his father's house.

This story, from Moses in the Book of Genesis, taught me a few things about the power of the mind and visualisation. Challenges like ill health and negative situations don't have to be permanent. One pathway to healing is to visualize what we want, instead of what we are experiencing. We can choose to prosper emotionally, mentally, physically and spiritually.

A few years ago, after I received the revelation that my body is a living organism with ears and that I must speak what I want to it, I began to visualise myself sharing the story of how I was healed to friends, family and even total strangers. At that time, my body was overwhelmed with excruciating pain, weakness, mood swings, food intolerances, low haemoglobin and myriad other ailments. I forced myself to see a healed me, joyful, free of pain and enjoying my life. It was difficult, but every morning I would stay in my bed until I had visualised what I wanted to see and feel. I continued until I felt the joy, excitement and inner peace. Today, that picture has become a reality. I share my stories with people everywhere, I give talks, provide workshops and I write about my healing journey.

What I'm trying to say here, my friend, is that what you see or imagine is what you will get. It doesn't matter what the situation is presently – sit down, take deep breaths and start visualising what you want, rather than what you do not want. One day, that dream will become a reality and you will also tell your story.

I am confident about this, not just because I have experienced it, but because the people I coach also experience it.

Everything you want is already in existence, even if you don't see it physically. Through your determination, you will see the manifestation of your prayers and wishes.

I look forward to seeing you in England soon, my dear Toriola.

Much love,

Wura xx

PS: I have listed below some of the books and articles that I found useful and relevant to the lessons I have shared in my letters. I do hope you enjoy reading them.

Recommended Books and Articles

Books

- Batmanghelidj, F. (2008) *Your Body's Many Cries for Water: You're Not Sick, You're Thirsty*. Global Health Solutions.

- Clayton, P. (2004) *Health Defence*. 2nd Edition. Accelerated Learning Systems Ltd.

- Erasmus, U. (1993) *Fats That Heal, Fats That Kill*. Alive Books.

- Fife, B. (2008) *Oil Pulling Therapy: Detoxifying and Healing the Body Through Oral Cleansing*. Piccadilly Books.

- Hills, M. (2012) *Treating Arthritis: The Drug Free Way*. Sheldon Press.

- Kharrazian, D. (2013) *Why Isn't My Brain Working?* Elephant Press.

- Leaf, C. (2013) *Switch on Your Brain: The Key to Peak Happiness, Thinking, and Health*. Baker Books.

- Lipski, E. (2001) *Digestive Wellness: Strengthen the Immune System and Prevent Disease Through Healthy Digestion*. McGraw Hill Contemporary.

- Mindlell, E. (2011) *Earl Mindell's New Vitamin Bible.* Warner Books Inc.
- Malkmus, G. (2005) *Why Christians Get Sick.* Destiny Image.
- Vernikos, J. (2011) *Sitting Kills, Moving Heals: How Everyday Movement Will Prevent Pain, Illness and Early Death.* Linden.
- Wigmore, A. (1987) *The Wheatgrass Book.* Avery.
- Wilson, K. (1996) *Anatomy and Physiology in Health and Illness.* Churchill Livingstone.

Articles

- Petrosino, J. and Snyder, M. (2014) 'What is your gut telling you?' [ONLINE] Available at: http://www.webmd.com/digestive-disorders/news/20140820/your-gut-bacteria.
- Pattanayak, S. and Sunita, P. (2011) 'Phytoestrogens in postmenopausal indications: A theoretical perspective' [ONLINE] Available at: http://www.ncbi.nlm.nih.gov/pmc/articles/PMC3210008/.
- Klein, S. (2010). 'Will you have your mother's menopause?' [ONLINE] Available at: http://edition.cnn.com/2010/HEALTH/07/17/mother.menopause/index.html.

- Hinterthuer, A. (2008) Just how harmful are bisphenol A plastics? [ONLINE] Available at: http://www.scientificamerican.com/article/just-how-harmful-are-bisphenol-a-plastics/.

About the Author

Abimbola is a researcher at Lapin yliopisto – University of Lapland, Finland. Her research explores the influence of psychosocial intervention for dementia care. Abimbola taught creative writing and storytelling at Plymouth Marjon University from 2007–2018. She is currently a visiting lecturer at the Peninsular Medical School, University of Plymouth, where she teaches 'Story Weavers for Dementia', a module in Medical Humanities.

Abimbola is an award-winning author, performance storyteller and playwright. Her short play *Legal Stuff* won the BBC and Royal Court Theatre's 24 Degrees Writing Competition in 2008. She is the author of *The Legendary Weaver: New Edition*, *Trickster Tales for Telling*, *The Goshen Principle* and *How to Enhance your Storytelling With Music.* Abimbola is also a children's book translator, and her work includes Yoruba translations of the classics 'Hansel and Gretel', 'The Little Red Hen and the Grain of Wheat', and several other books published by Mantra Lingua.

www.abimbolaalao.com

www.facebook.com/storytellerabimbola

Other Books by Abimbola Gbemi Alao

The Goshen Principle: A Shelter in the Time of Storm
By Abimbola Gbemi Alao

ISBN
Paperback: 9780954625511
Ebook: 9780954625559

The Legendary Weaver: New Edition
By Abimbola Gbemi Alao

ISBN
9780954625528

How to Enhance Your Storytelling with Music
By Abimbola Gbemi Alao

ISBN
Paperback: 978-0-954625535
Ebook: 978-0-954625566

Trickster Tales for Telling
By Abimbola Gbemi Alao

ISBN
Paperback: 978-0-954625542
Ebook: 978-0-954625573

Dual Language books, translated by Abimbola Gbemi Alao

Floppy's Friends: 'Awon ore e Floppy'
Dual Language Yoruba translation by Abimbola Alao. (2004) Mantra Lingua.

ISBN
1 84444240 3

Hansel and Gretel: 'Hansel ati Gretel'
Dual Language Yoruba translation by Abimbola Alao. (2005) Mantra Lingua.

ISBN
1 84444778 2

The little Red Hen and the Grains of Wheat: 'Adie Pupa Kekere ati Eso Alikama'
Dual Language Yoruba translation by Abimbola Alao. (2005) Mantra Lingua.

ISBN
1 84444219 5

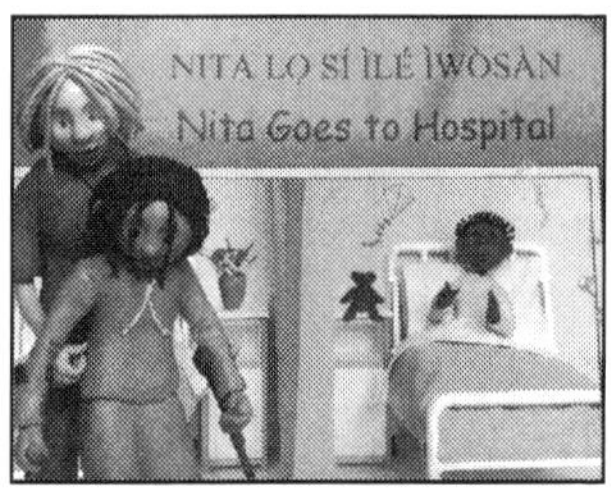

Nita Goes to Hospital: 'Nita lo si ile iwosan'
Dual Language Yoruba translation by Abimbola Alao. (2005) Mantra Lingua.

ISBN
1 84444836 3

Grandma's Saturday Soup:
'Obe Ojo Abameta Mama Agba'
Dual Language Yoruba translation by Abimbola Alao. (2005) Mantra Lingua.

ISBN
1 84444951 3

Welcome to the world baby:
'Kaabo sinu aye Omo titun'
Dual Language Yoruba translation by Abimbola Alao. (2005) Mantra Lingua.

ISBN
1 84444297 7

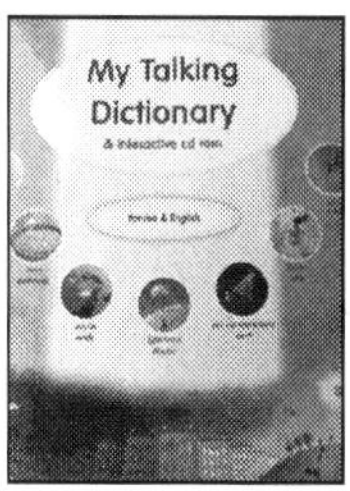

My Talking Dictionary & Interactive CD ROM
Yoruba & English - Yoruba translation by Abimbola Alao. (2005) Mantra Lingua.

ISBN
1 84444717 0

Printed in Great Britain
by Amazon

66411003R00078